Succeed on the Standardized Test

This Book Includes:

- 3 Practice tests that mirror the standardized test
- Answer key and Detailed explanations
- Writing Tasks, Reading Tasks, Language Skills
- Strategies for building speed and accuracy
- Content aligned with the new Common Core State Standards

Plus access to Online Workbooks, which include:

- Hundreds of practice questions
- Individualized score reports
- Instant feedback after completion of the workbook
- Self paced learning

Complement Classroom Learning All Year

Using the Lumos Study Program, parents and teachers can reinforce the classroom learning experience for children. It creates a collaborative learning platform for students, teachers and parents.

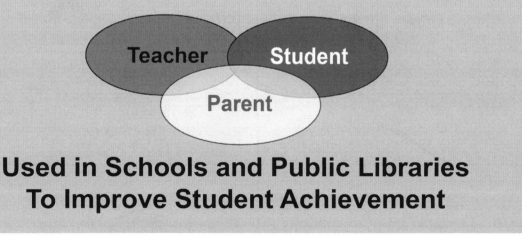

Used in Schools and Public Libraries To Improve Student Achievement

Lumos Learning

Common Core Assessments and Online Workbooks: Grade 6 Language Arts and Literacy, PARCC Edition

Contributing Editor	- **Janet Redell**
Contributing Editor	- **Lisa Calamari**
Contributing Editor	- **Asher Brown**
Contributing Editor	- **Kia Simmons**
Contributing Editor	- **Lisa Calamari**
Editor	- **George Smith**
Curriculum Director	- **Marisa Adams**
Executive Producer	- **Mukunda Krishnaswamy**
Designer and Illustrator	- **Mirona Jova**

ISBN-10: 1940484154

ISBN-13: 978-1-940484-15-0

Printed in the United States of America

For permissions and additional information contact us

Lumos Information Services, LLC
PO Box 1575, Piscataway, NJ 08855-1575
http://www.LumosLearning.com

Email: support@lumoslearning.com
Tel: (732) 384-0146
Fax: (866) 283-6471

Lumos Learning

Table of Contents

Introduction

The Common Core State Standards Initiative (CCSS) was created from the need to have more robust and rigorous guidelines, standardized from state to state. These guidelines create a learning environment where students will be able to graduate high school with all skills necessary to be active and successful members of society, whether they take a role in the workforce or in some sort of post secondary education.

How Can the Lumos Study Program Impact Student Success?
Beginning in the spring of 2014, student mastery of Common Core State Standards will be assessed using standardized testing methods. At Lumos Learning, we believe that year long learning and adequate practice before the actual test are the keys to success on these standardized tests. We have designed the Lumos study program to help students get plenty of realistic practice before the test and to promote year long collaborative learning.

Inside this book, you will find three full-length practice tests that are similar to the standardized tests students will take to assess their mastery of CCSS aligned curriculum. Completing these tests will help students master the different areas that are included in newly aligned standardized tests and practice test taking skills. The results will help the students and educators get insights into students' strengths and weaknesses in specific content areas. These insights could be used to help students strengthen their skills in difficult topics and to improve speed and accuracy while taking the test.

This is a Lumos **tedBook**™! It connects you to Online Workbooks and additional resources using a number of devices including android phones, iPhones, tablets and personal compuers. The Lumos StepUp Online Workbooks are designed to promote year long learning. It is a simple program students can securely access using a computer or device with internet access. It consists of hundreds of grade appropriate questions, aligned to the new Common Core State Standards. Students will get instant feedback and can review their answers anytime. Each student's answers and progress can be reviewed by parents and educators to reinforce the learning experience.

How to use this book effectively

The Lumos Program is a flexible learning tool. It can be adapted to suit a student's skill level and the time available to practice before standardized tests. Here are some tips to help you use this book and the online workbooks effectively:

Students
- You can use the "Diagnostic Test" to understand your mastery of different topics and test taking skills.
- Use the "Related Lumos StepUp Online Workbook" in the Answer Key section to identify the topic that is related to each question.
- Use the Online workbooks to practice your areas of difficulty and complement classroom learning.
- Download the Lumos StepUp app using the instructions provided to have anywhere access to online resources.
- Have open-ended questions evaluated by a teacher or parent keeping in mind the scoring rubrics.
- Take the "Practice Tests" as you get close to the standardized tests date.
- Complete the test in a quiet place, following the test guidelines. Practice tests provide you an opportunity to improve your test taking skills and to review topics included in the standardized tests.

Parents
- Familiarize yourself with the test format and expectations.
- Help your child use Lumos StepUp Online Workbooks by following the instructions in "How to access the Lumos Online Workbooks" section of this chapter.
- Help your student download the Lumos StepUp app using the instructions provided in "How to download the Lumos StepUp App" section of this chapter.
- Review your child's performance in the "Lumos Online Workbooks" periodically. You can do this by simply asking your child to log into the system online and selecting the subject area you wish to review.
- Review your child's work in the Practice Tests.
- Visit http://lumoslearning.com/a/parents to learn more.

Teachers
- Please contact **support@lumoslearning.com** to request a **teacher account.** A teacher account will help you create custom assessments and lessons as well as review the online work of your students. Visit **http://www.lumoslearning.com/lal-quill** to learn more.
- Download the Lumos StepUp app using the instructions provided to get convenient access to Common Core State Standards and additional resources.
- If your school has purchased the school edition of this book, please use this book as the Teacher Guide.
- You can use the Lumos online programs along with this book to complement and extend your classroom instruction.

     LumosLearning.com

PARCC Frequently Asked Questions

What is PARCC?

The Partnership for Assessment of Readiness and College and Careers (PARCC) is one of two state consortiums responsible for developing assessments aligned to the new, more rigorous Common Core State Standards. There are currently 20 states involved in the PARCC consortium and a combination of educational leaders from those states along with test developers are working together to create the new computer based English Language Arts and Math assessments..

When is the PARCC Timeline?

Currently, PARCC is set to deliver the new assessments for the 2014-2015 school year. Most states are utilizing their own state assessments, realigned to meet new PARCC guidelines for the 2013-2014 school year. Sample test items will be released throughout the 2013-2014 school year, and a full sample test will be available in the spring of 2014.

Is this book completely aligned with the PARCC assessment guidelines?

Many clients question if PARCC is still in the process of creating a testing framework, how can there be a PARCC aligned book. This is a valid concern during this transition year.

This PARCC tedBook is aligned to the Common Core State Standards. Most states that are in the PARCC consortium will measure student achievement through state tests in the Spring of 2014 and PARCC assessments in the 2014-2015 academic year. This book is designed to assist students and teachers during the transitional assessment period. Once PARCC releases the final assessment guidelines, the book will be reformatted to continue assessing CCSS through the new PARCC assessment format.

What are the planned parts of PARCC assessments?

Although still in design phase, PARCC has released a plan for the yearly assessments. They will consist of:
• Optional diagnostic assessment
• Mid-year assessment
• Performance-based assessment
• End of year assessment
• Speaking and listening component assessment

Where can I get more information about PARCC?

You can obtain up-to-date information on PARCC, including sample assessment items, schedules, & the answers to frequently asked questions from the PARCC website at http://www.parcconline.org

Where can I get additional information about the Common Core State Standards (CCSS)?

Please visit http://www.corestandards.org/ELA-Literacy

How to access the Lumos Online Workbooks

First Time Access:
Using a computer with internet access, go to
http://www.LumosLearning.com/book

Enter the following access code in the Access Code field and press the Submit button.

Access Code: CG6L-954-2511

In the next screen, click on the "New User" button to register your user name and password.

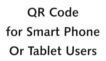

QR Code
for Smart Phone
Or Tablet Users

Subsequent Access:
After you establish your user id and password for subsequent access, simply login with your account information.

What if I buy more than one Lumos Study Program?
Please note that you can use all Online Workbooks with one User ID and Password. If you buy more than one book, you will access them with the same account.
Go back to the http://www.LumosLearning.com/book link and enter the access code provided in the second book. In the next screen simply login using your previously created account.

Lumos StepUp™ Mobile App FAQ

What is the Lumos StepUp App?

It is a FREE application you can download onto your android smart phones, tablets, iPhones, and iPads.

What are the Benefits of the StepUp App?

This mobile application gives convenient access to Common Core State Standards, Practice Tests and StepUp Online Workbooks through your smart phone and tablet computers.

Do I Need the StepUp App to Access Online Workbooks?

No, you can access Lumos StepUp Online Workbooks through a personal computer. The StepUp app simply enhances your learning experience and allows you to conveniently access StepUp Online Workbooks and additional resources through your smart phone or tablet.

How can I Download the App?

Visit **http://LumosLearning.com/a/apps** using your smart phone or tablet and follow the instructions to download the app.

**QR Code
for Smart Phone
Or Tablet Users**

Test Taking Tips

1) **The day before the test**, make sure you get a good night's sleep.

2) **On the day of the test**, be sure to eat a good hearty breakfast! Also, be sure to arrive at school on-time.

3) **During the test:**

Read every question carefully.

While Answering Multiple-Choice questions:

- Do not circle the answer choices. Fill in the bubble corresponding to your answer choice.
- Read **all** of the answer choices, even if think you have found the correct answer.
- Do not spend too much time on any one question. Work steadily through all questions in the section.
- Attempt all of the questions even if you are not sure of some answers.
- If you run into a difficult question, eliminate as many choices as you can and then pick the best one from the remaining choices. Intelligent guessing will help you increase your score.
- Also, mark the question so that if you have extra time, you can return to it after you reach the end of the section. Try to erase the marks after you complete the work.
- Some questions may refer to a graph, chart, or other kind of picture. Carefully review the graphic before answering the question.

While Answering Open-ended questions:

- Open-ended questions typically have multiple parts. Make sure you answer **all** parts clearly.
- Be sure to include explanations for your written responses and show all work.
- Some questions may refer to a graph, chart, or other kind of picture. Carefully review the graphic before answering the question.

Diagnostic Test

Student Name:

Test Date:

Start Time:

End Time:

Writing Task 1

Here are some reminders for when you are completing this Writing Task:

- Using the situation given below as a guide, write a story in your own words.
- You may take notes, create a web, or do other prewriting work. Then, write your story on a sheet of paper.
- After you complete writing your composition, read whatever you have written. Make sure that your writing is the best it can be.

Writing Situation: The park in your area has only one tennis court. It is always crowded and one has to wait at least two hours before getting a chance to play.

Writing Task: Write a persuasive letter to your mayor requesting more tennis courts in your area. In your letter, be sure to describe the situation and explain the reasons why you need more tennis courts.

Prewriting Area

Writing Task 1

Reading Task 1

Directions to the Student

Now you will read a story and answer the questions that follow.
Some questions will be multiple-choice; others will be open-ended.

- You may look back at the reading passage as often as you want.
- Read each question carefully and think about the answer and fill in the circle completely next to your choice.
- If you do not know the answer to a question, go on to the next question and come back to the skipped question later.

The Big Dessert Showdown

"Again, I would like to thank all of the aspiring young chefs who participated in our Future Chefs of America competition. And now the 3 finalists who will be joining us for tomorrow's big dessert showdown are..." Rachel trembled uncontrollably as she waited for Chef Rubin to announce the names of the finalists. Finally, Chef Rubin looked out into the audience and said, "Our 3 finalists are Alex Williams from New York, David Wu from Texas, and..." Chef Rubin paused for what seemed like an eternity to the contestants and then said, "And Rachel Green from New Jersey!" The roar of the crowd helped prevent Rachel from fainting at the sound of her name.

"Congratulations to our 3 finalists, and I hope everyone will join us tomorrow for the big dessert showdown," exclaimed Chef Rubin.

"Rachel, we are so proud of you!" said her dad as he drove back to the hotel.

"Yes we really are!" her mom interjected. "Have you decided what dessert you're going to make in the showdown?" "Not yet," sighed Rachel. "I'm still thinking."

When they reached the hotel, Rachel's parents decided to order a pizza and go to bed early. They wanted to make sure Rachel was well rested and ready for the big showdown. Although Rachel turned in early, she had trouble falling asleep. She worried about choosing the wrong dessert and not impressing the judges. Then she panicked at the thought of having to compete against David Wu. His dad is a world-renowned chef and David had traveled the globe learning cooking techniques in some of the most famous kitchens.

"What am I going to make? How will I ever win this contest?" Rachel mumbled as she drifted off to sleep.

"Rachel, do you remember the fun we always had in the kitchen?" asked a pleasantly familiar voice. Rachel couldn't see the person through the blinding light.

"Grandma Ella, is that you?"

"Yes, Lemon Drop. This is your Grandma."

"Hi, Grandma!" said Rachel as she choked back tears. "How did you—?"

Grandma Ella interrupted and said "Rachel, I want you to do me a favor. Just relax. Don't worry about the other competitors. Don't worry about trying to make a dessert that will impress the judges. Just remember the fun we always had together while cooking. Just have fun in the kitchen tomorrow."

The next morning, Rachel got up bright and early. She felt relaxed and ready to compete in the big dessert showdown.

"Rachel, I guess getting some extra pizza really helped?" said her Dad.

"Yes, Dad, replied Rachel. "I never felt better!"

Before the big competition began, Rachel wished David and Alex good luck. She happily hummed and at times looked as if she was dancing while making her dessert.

An hour and a half later, the desserts were finished and ready to be judged.

"Now, the time has finally arrived!" exclaimed Chef Rubin. "Drum roll please."

"Our next Future Chef of America is Rachel Green from New Jersey!" bellowed Chef Rubin.

As the confetti fell, Rachel stepped up to accept her trophy. "Rachel, your lemon drop cookies were just amazing," Chef Rubin said. "Tell us, where did you get your recipe?"

Rachel smiled and said, "It's just a simple recipe my Grandma Ella taught me."

1. Based on the passage, how does the reader know the competitors are from different states around the country?

   Ⓐ Chef Rubin calls the competitors "aspiring young chefs."
   Ⓑ Chef Rubin announces the name of the state each competitor is from.
   Ⓒ The name of the contest is Future Chefs of America.
   Ⓓ Chef Rubin says the winner will be from America.

2. What don't Rachel's parents do to help her get ready for the big showdown?

   Ⓐ They go directly to the hotel after the cooking competition.
   Ⓑ They have dinner with Rachel in the hotel room.
   Ⓒ The family goes to bed early.
   Ⓓ They stay up all night helping Rachel decide on a recipe.

3. Which statement is not a reason given as to why Rachel is worried about competing against David Wu?

   Ⓐ He is the son of a famous chef.
   Ⓑ He knows cooking techniques from around the world.
   Ⓒ He has cooked with famous chefs.
   Ⓓ He is a talented cook.

4. Which phrase helps the reader know that Rachel was dreaming about her Grandma Ella?

   Ⓐ drifted off to sleep
   Ⓑ see the person through the blinding light
   Ⓒ pleasantly familiar voice
   Ⓓ yes, lemon Drop

5. What is the theme of the story?

   Ⓐ Trust your family
   Ⓑ Do not stress
   Ⓒ Practice makes perfect
   Ⓓ Remember family memories

6. Why does Rachel hum and look as if she was dancing while making her dessert?

   Ⓐ She likes to sing and dance.
   Ⓑ She doesn't take her Grandma Ella's advice.
   Ⓒ She's having fun in the kitchen.
   Ⓓ She's making her least favorite recipe

7. Why did Rachel tremble as she waited for Chef Rubin to announce the names of the three finalists?

    Ⓐ She was angry.
    Ⓑ She was nervous.
    Ⓒ She was tired.
    Ⓓ She had an illness that caused her tremble.

8. Why does Rachel decide to make lemon drop cookies?

    Ⓐ Her parents told her to make them.
    Ⓑ Her grandmother told her to make them.
    Ⓒ She wanted to honor her grandmother's memory.
    Ⓓ She wanted to impress the judges.

Open-Ended Question 1

Here are some reminders for when you are completing this Open-Ended Question:

- Read the passage "The Big Dessert Showdown" and the open-ended question and write your answer on a sheet of paper.
- Focus your response on the question asked.
- Answer all parts of the question and explain your answer with specific details.
- Use specific information from the story to answer all the parts of the question.

9. **In The Big Dessert Showdown, Rachel said she just followed a simple recipe that her grandmother taught her.**

- **Describe what you think Rachel means by this statement.**
- **Discuss how Rachel's dream helped her win the big competition.**
- **Explain why the ingredients Rachel used in her winning recipe have little to do with the actual food.**

Writing Task 2

Here are some reminders for when you are completing this Writing Task:

- Using the situation given below as a guide, write a story in your own words.
- You may take notes, create a web, or do other prewriting work.
- After you complete writing your composition, read whatever you have written. Make sure that your writing is the best it can be.

Writing Situation: Do you have something that is especially important to you? It could be something you found, made, or has been given to you.

Writing Task: Write an essay describing what this item is and explain why it is important to you.

Prewriting Area

  LumosLearning.com

Writing Task 2

LumosLearning.com

Reading Task 2

Directions to the Student

Now you will read another passage and answer the questions that follow.
Some questions will be multiple-choice; others will be open-ended.

- You may look back at the reading passage as often as you want.
- Read each question carefully and think about the answer and completely fill in the circle next to your choice.
- If you do not know the answer to a question, go on to the next question and come back to the skipped question later.

Two Related Bat-and-Ball Games

I was born in Mumbai, India where the sport of cricket is very popular. As a young child, I would often play cricket with my dad, other family members and friends. I would have to say that other than field hockey, cricket was one of my favorite sports to play in my homeland.

When I was 10 years old, my family moved to the United States. We lived in Edison, New Jersey, and I made many new friends there. Baseball was one of the first games my new friends taught me how to play. After learning how to play baseball, I wasn't surprised that I enjoyed playing baseball just as much as I enjoyed playing cricket.

Baseball and cricket are two of the best-known related bat-and-ball games, they have many similaritites. The most obvious similarity is that both baseball and cricket are played with a bat and a ball. Each sport has a person who throws the ball to a batter and a batter who tries to hit the ball. In baseball, this person is the pitcher, but in cricket, this person is called the bowler. Also in both games, there are defensive and offensive features. In cricket, the batsman is attempting to defend the wicket. In baseball, the batter wants to defend the strike zone.

Despite their similarities, the two sports also have many differences. There are eleven players on a team in cricket while a baseball team has nine players. Baseball players use thin, round bats and wear gloves to field, while cricketers use wide, flat bats and only the wicket-keeper wears gloves. Another difference between the two sports is the batting order. The batting order in baseball must be declared before the game begins, and can only be changed if a substitution occurs. When a baseball team's manager makes a substitution, the new player must occupy the same place in the batting order as the old one, otherwise the team is in violation and will be penalized for batting out of turn. However unlike baseball, the batting order in cricket is not fixed, and can be changed at any time, as long as each player bats at least once.

Also, baseball games are generally much shorter than cricket games. A typical professional baseball game can last between two and one-half and four and one-half hours. However, if you are playing a version of cricket known as Test cricket, the games can last up to five days with scheduled breaks each day for lunch and tea. The shorter version of the Test cricket game is called "one-day games" and usually lasts from five to seven hours, but can sometimes continue for longer than eight hours.

Both cricket and baseball represent a special part of who I am. I learned how to play cricket on native soil while I learned how to play baseball in my other homeland. I feel lucky to say that I enjoy and know how to play both sports very well.

LumosLearning.com

10. Who is a bowler?

Ⓐ the batter in a baseball game
Ⓑ the umpire in a baseball game
Ⓒ the batter in a cricket game
Ⓓ the pitcher in a cricket game

11. Which statement about the batting order in baseball is not true?

Ⓐ The batting order in baseball is fixed.
Ⓑ The batting order in baseball must be announced before the game begins.
Ⓒ The team will not be in violation if the order is changed.
Ⓓ The team will receive a violation if they bat out of turn.

12. Which statement about the length of a cricket game is not true?

Ⓐ A game of cricket is always shorter than a game of baseball.
Ⓑ A game of cricket can last for up to five days.
Ⓒ A game of cricket can involve taking breaks for lunch and tea.
Ⓓ A game of cricket can last for longer than eight hours.

13. How does the reader know the narrator enjoys living in America?

Ⓐ The narrator calls America his other homeland.
Ⓑ The narrator likes the game of baseball.
Ⓒ The narrator says he feels lucky.
Ⓓ The narrator likes the game of cricket.

14. This passage is:

Ⓐ Poetry
Ⓑ Nonfiction
Ⓒ Realistic fiction
Ⓓ Persuasive essay

15. Where is the narrator's homeland?

Ⓐ Edison, New Jersey
Ⓑ Mumbai, India
Ⓒ New Jersey, Edison
Ⓓ India, Mumbai

16. Who taught the narrator how to play baseball?

Ⓐ His dad
Ⓑ His family members
Ⓒ His new friends in Edison
Ⓓ His friends from Mumbai

17. One way cricket and baseball are alike is

Ⓐ Both sports are played with a ball and a bat.
Ⓑ Neither sports have a pitcher.
Ⓒ Both sports have defensive features only.
Ⓓ Neither sport has offensive features.

18. The wicket in a cricket game is similar to

Ⓐ the bat in a baseball game.
Ⓑ the gloves in a baseball game.
Ⓒ the strike zone in a baseball game.
Ⓓ the bowler in a cricket game.

LumosLearning.com

Open-Ended Question 2

Here are some reminders for when you are completing this Open-Ended Question:

- Read the passage "Two Related Bat-And-Ball Games" and the open-ended question and write your answer on a sheet of paper.
- Focus your response on the question asked.
- Answer all parts of the question and explain your answer with specific details.
- Use specific information from the story to answer all the parts of the question.

19. In the passage, the narrator feels lucky to say that he enjoys and knows how to play both sports very well.

- Describe why you think the author does not like playing one game more than the other.
- Discuss why the narrator calls America his other homeland.
- Explain why you think the narrator feels lucky.

Reading Task 3

Directions to the Student

Now you will read another passage and answer the questions that follow. Some questions will be multiple-choice; others will be open-ended.

- You may look back at the reading passage as often as you want.
- Read each question carefully and think about the answer and completely fill in the circle next to your choice.
- If you do not know the answer to a question, go on to the next question and come back to the skipped question later.

My Wish

Latin class @ 3:00
Piano lesson @ 4:00
Then play rehearsal and finally homework
With this schedule, life's never a bore.
But sometimes I wish
I wish that I could be free
Free to think
Free to daydream
Free to just be me!
A kid with no commitments
Well, other than school
And maybe one extracurricular activity
That I get to choose
Yes, sometimes I wish
I wish that I could be free
Free to think
Free to daydream
Free to just be me!

By Kia Simmons

20. **Why does the author wish that she could be free?**

Ⓐ because she has very hectic schedule and has no time to even think
Ⓑ because she has been kept captive and she is tired of it
Ⓒ because she has been doing many things and she wants to do some more
Ⓓ because she just wants to think and daydream

21. **"And maybe one extracurricular activity"**

What does the word "extracurricular" mean according to the above poem?

Ⓐ Outside the conventional bounds
Ⓑ Outside the regular curriculum
Ⓒ Outside one's capacity
Ⓓ Outside activity

22. **What is the poet's schedule like?**

Ⓐ Latin Class @ 3:00 pm, homework, play rehearsal
Ⓑ Latin Class @ 3:00 pm, Piano class @ 4:00 pm
Ⓒ Latin class @ 3:00 pm, Piano class @ 4:00 pm, play rehearsal dinner and sleep
Ⓓ Latin class @ 3:00 pm, Piano class @ 4:00 pm, play rehearsal and then homework

23. **What does the poet wish her schedule would be like?**

Ⓐ No commitments, other than school and one extracurricular activity
Ⓑ No commitments
Ⓒ School and Piano lessons
Ⓓ More play rehearsals to go with the piano lessons

24. **What is the main idea of the above poem?**

Ⓐ Kids need time to be just themselves every day
Ⓑ Kids need time to just think and daydream
Ⓒ Both A and B
Ⓓ Kids need plenty to do

25. **What details in the above poem tell us that the poet is a child who is very involved in activities both in and out of school?**

Ⓐ Then play rehearsal and finally homework
Ⓑ And maybe one extracurricular activity, that I get to choose
Ⓒ A kid with no commitments, well, other than school
Ⓓ All of these

    LumosLearning.com

26. Which detail in the above passage tells us that the poet does not have any free time?

Ⓐ But sometimes I wish, I wish that I could be free, free to think, free to daydream, free to just be me!

Ⓑ Latin class @ 3:00, Piano lesson @ 4:00, Then play rehearsal and finally homework

Ⓒ A kid with no commitments, well, other than school

Ⓓ And maybe one extracurricular activity, that I get to choose

27. What does the poet want to do in the free time?

Ⓐ The poet wants to day dream.

Ⓑ The poet wants to do more.

Ⓒ The poet wants to write poetry.

Ⓓ The poet wants to learn art.

Open-Ended Question 3

Here are some reminders for when you are completing this Open-Ended Question:
• Read the passage "My Wish" and the open-ended question and write your answer on a sheet of paper.
• Focus your response on the question asked.
• Answer all parts of the question and explain your answer with specific details.
• Use specific information from the story to answer all the parts of the question.

28. After reading the above poem:

- •Describe what your schedule is on a daily basis.
- •Discuss the similarities and differences between your schedule and the poet's schedule.
- •Explain what you would wish to do if you had the free time.

Reading Task 4

Directions to the Student

Now you will read a story and answer the questions that follow.
Some questions will be multiple-choice; others will be open-ended.

- You may look back at the reading passage as often as you want.
- Read each question carefully and think about the answer and completely fill in the circle next to your choice.
- If you do not know the answer to a question, go on to the next question and come back to the skipped question later.

Unlikely Heroes

Heroes come in many forms, shapes and sizes, but would you ever think of worms as heroes? In the 17th century, doctors believed that many illnesses and diseases could be cured by bloodletting or draining people's blood. When bloodletting, doctors attached blood-sucking worms known as leeches to the bodies of their patients to drain out the blood. Both the doctors and the patients liked the fact that doctors were able to control how much blood was sucked by the leeches and that they didn't need to cut open their patients with knives. Also, leeches were easily found in ponds and streams all over Europe. By the early 1800's London hospitals used approximately 7 million leeches per year to treat almost everything from headaches and mental illness to obesity.

In modern medicine, bloodletting is no longer practiced, but doctors still understand the benefits of using leeches in many medical procedures. For example, surgeons will often use leeches to drain extra blood after reattaching body parts that have been cut off. This procedure is almost pain-free because leeches have an anesthetic in their saliva. Leeches have also been used as blood thinners to reduce the blood accumulation in body tissues after plastic surgery. In 2004, Douglas Cephora, a surgeon at the University of Michigan, stated in a USA Today news report that he treats about three patients a year with leeches after reconstructing faces or mouths destroyed by cancer. Leeches used in surgical procedures cannot be reapplied and are disposed of like hypodermic needles. Proper disposal of used leeches helps prevent the spread of diseases such as AIDS, which is carried in the bloodstream.

Scientists are currently studying other chemicals in leech saliva because they think these chemicals can be used to make life-saving drugs. However, to conduct the necessary research, scientists need huge amounts of leech saliva. Breeding leeches has become one way scientists are able to obtain the massive amounts of leeches needed for medical purposes. Today, the British company, BioPharm, provides thousands of leeches each year to hospitals in countries around the world.

LumosLearning.com

Although many people have fears and may even squirm at the thought of being treated by blood-sucking leeches, they understand the value of medical leeches and they know that leeches have been used throughout history to save human lives.

29. The purpose of the first paragraph is to

Ⓐ encourage the reader to study leeches
Ⓑ inform the reader of how leeches were used by doctors long ago
Ⓒ inform the reader about the dangers of bloodletting
Ⓓ explain the physical characteristics of a hero

30. Based on the passage, in what types of habitats can most leeches be found?

Ⓐ Near plants
Ⓑ Aquatic areas
Ⓒ Pet stores
Ⓓ Flying through the air

31. Based on the passage, which statement would not be true?

Ⓐ Leech saliva produces several useful chemicals.
Ⓑ Leeches can be used as blood thinners.
Ⓒ Leeches can be reused during surgical procedures.
Ⓓ Leeches have been used after reconstructing faces or mouths destroyed by cancer.

32. According to the passage, why do scientists need huge amounts of leech saliva?

Ⓐ They are selling the leech saliva to sick patients.
Ⓑ The leech saliva is needed for scientific research.
Ⓒ Leech saliva can spoil if it's not used right away.
Ⓓ Leeches can be easily bred.

33. In the third paragraph, what does the word "breeding" mean?

Ⓐ Selling
Ⓑ Killing
Ⓒ Planting
Ⓓ Reproducing

34. Who would most benefit from the use of medical leeches?

Ⓐ A man who had his finger reattached after it was cut off.
Ⓑ A woman who develops a blood clot during surgery.
Ⓒ A child who just had reconstructive surgery on his face.
Ⓓ All of the above.

35. Why do you think doctors no longer practice bloodletting?

    Ⓐ The procedure is too expensive
    Ⓑ Draining blood isn't an effective treatment for most diseases.
    Ⓒ Leeches became an endangered species.
    Ⓓ Using leeches became too unpredictable.

36. What does the word "anesthetic" mean in the second paragraph?

    Ⓐ Painkiller
    Ⓑ Solution
    Ⓒ Blood Thinner
    Ⓓ Antibiotic

37. Why do you think a surgeon use leeches to drain off extra blood after reattaching severed body parts?

    Ⓐ It can help produce more leeches.
    Ⓑ Doctors need a forceful way to drain off excess blood.
    Ⓒ Swelling can occur in the reattached body part if the extra blood is not drained.
    Ⓓ Swelling from a reattached body part is only relieved through leeches.

Open-Ended Question 4

Here are some reminders for when you are completing this Open-Ended Question:

- Read the passage "Unlikely Heroes" and the open-ended question and write your answer on a sheet of paper.
- Focus your response on the question asked.
- Answer all parts of the question and explain your answer with specific details.
- Use specific information from the story to answer all the parts of the question.

38. **This passage described why medical leeches can be considered heroes.**

- **Discuss whether or not you agree that medical leeches can be considered heroes.**
- **Describe how you think medical treatments that use leeches would be affected if leeches became extinct.**
- **Explain some other ways you think doctors might use leeches in the future.**

End Of Diagnostic Test

Diagnostic Test Answers

Sample Answer for Writing Task 1

A 5-point response should include

- Answers to all parts of the question
- Reference to the text in the response
- Personal comparisons

Dear Mayor,

I know you are very busy, but there is an Important Issue I would like to address with you. The park in my neighborhood doesn't have enough tennis courts to accommodate all of the people who want to use them. Almost everyone in my neighborhood enjoys playing tennis, but there is only one court for all of us to share. Sometimes we have to wait hours to play. That is especially hard for the younger kids who have early curfews. By the time they have a chance to play, they have to go home.

First, most of us need to wait hours to play tennis because there is only one court. This is inconvenient because we all try to come and play after school, and instead of getting to have some fun after school, we are waiting for hours to play one game. Tennis is a great way to keep kids active instead of them sitting on a couch and playing video games. Adding additional courts will help solve both these problems and keep the kids in your town active and healthy.

Next, the younger kids who want to play often have to go home before they even have the opportunity to get one game in. The parents enjoy knowing their kids are at the tennis courts and do not worry about them. However, if they continue having to wait so long, they may get bored and do something else, which may get them in trouble. Having a safe place for the kids to go is important.

I know that the budget is tight this year, but I think that an additional tennis court would be a good investment for the neighborhood. Tennis is a great sport to play with friends and family. It helps keep us out of trouble by giving us something positive to do with our time. It helps keep us in shape and helps us learn friendly competition. When we play doubles, it also helps us learn to work in teams.

I understand if you are not able to add another tennis court at our park, but I hope you will at least consider it. It would be good for our whole community.

Sincerely,
Tommy Brown
Grade 6

Related Lumos Online Workbook: Correct Use of Adjectives and Adverbs; Correct Subject-Verb Agreement; Recognize Pronouns; Demonstrate Command of Capitalization; Demonstrate Command of Punctuation; Correct Spelling (CCSS: L.6.1, L.6.2, L.6.3)

Reading Task 1 Answer Key

Question No.	Answer	Related Lumos Online Workbook	CCSS
1	B	Analysis of Key Events and Ideas	RL.6.1
2	D	Analysis of Key Events and Ideas	RL.6.1
3	D	Analysis of Key Events and Ideas	RL.6.1
4	A	Figurative Words and Phrases; Connotative Words and Phrases; Meaning of Words and Phrases	RL.6.4
5	B	Figurative Words and Phrases; Connotative Words and Phrases; Meaning of Words and Phrases	RL.6.4
6	C	Development of Ideas; Summary of Text; Figurative Words and Phrases; Connotative Words and Phrases; Meaning of Words and Phrases	RL.6.2, RL.6.4
7	B	Analysis of Key Events and Ideas	RL.6.1
8	C	Development of Ideas; Overall Development of Ideas	RL.6.5

Sample Answer for Open–Ended Question 1

A 4-point response should include:
- Answer to all parts of the question
- Reference to the text in response
- Personal comparisons

When Rachel said she was following a recipe her grandmother taught her, she was talking about the fun of baking (not the actual ingredients in the recipe). Her dream helped her win because her grandmother reminded her how much fun they used to have when they baked together. It also helped because her grandmother called her "lemon drop," which gave her the idea for what type of dessert she should make.

Rachel's cookies won the contest because she made them with lots of joy and was relaxed enough to have fun while she was baking. The judges could sense that she loved cooking, and that the cookies were made with love. Sometimes the spirit you use to do something is just as important as things like the actual ingredients. The same can be said for almost anything in life – the spirit with which you approach something will determine how well it turns out. Rachel truly enjoyed baking because of what her grandmother and followed her simple recipe to help her win.

Related Lumos Online Workbook: Correct Use of Adjectives and Adverbs; Correct Subject-Verb Agreement; Recognize Pronouns; Demonstrate Command of Capitalization; Demonstrate Command of Punctuation; Correct Spelling (CCSS: L.6.1, L.6.2, L.6.3)

Sample Answer for Writing Task 2

A 5-point response should include
- Answers to all parts of the question
- Reference to the text in the response
- Personal comparisons

One of the most important things I have is a ring that my mom gave to me when my grandmother died. The ring belonged to my grandmother. My grandfather gave it to her when they were dating. My mom had been keeping it for me until I was old enough to wear it. She said that I was so strong and brave when my grandma died that I deserved to have it earlier than she expected.

The ring is gold and has an opal in it. Even though it is old, it sparkles in the light. Sometimes I like to look at it and imagine my grandma seeing it sparkle up in heaven. I can imagine how it would have looked when she wore it.

My mom told me that the things that are passed on to us from our parents and grandparents are some of the most important things we will ever receive. For that reason I will always treasure it, and hopefully one day I can pass it on to my daughter.

Related Lumos Online Workbook: Correct Use of Adjectives and Adverbs; Correct Subject-Verb Agreement; Recognize Pronouns; Demonstrate Command of Capitalization; Demonstrate Command of Punctuation; Correct Spelling (CCSS: L.6.1, L.6.2, L.6.3)

Reading Task 2 Answer Key

Question No.	Answer	Related Lumos Online Workbook	CCSS
10	D	Analysis of Key Events and Ideas; Conclusions Drawn from the Text	RI.6.1
11	C	Analysis of Key Events and Ideas; Conclusions Drawn from the Text	RI.6.1
12	A	Analysis of Key Events and Ideas; Conclusions Drawn from the Text	RI.6.1
13	D	Analysis of Key Events and Ideas; Summary of Text; Central Idea of the Text	RI.6.3, RI.6.5
14	C	Analysis of Key Events and Ideas; Conclusions Drawn from the Text	RI.6.1
15	C	Analysis of Key Events and Ideas; Conclusions Drawn from the Text	RI.6.1
16	C	Analysis of Key Events and Ideas; Conclusions Drawn from the Text	RI.6.1
17	A	Analysis of Key Events and Ideas; Conclusions Drawn from the Text	RI.6.1
18	C	Analysis of Key Events and Ideas; Conclusions Drawn from the Text	RI.6.1

LumosLearning.com

Sample Answer for Open-Ended Question 2

A 4-point response should include:
- Answers to all parts of the question
- Reference to the text in the response
- Personal comparisons

The author does not enjoy playing one game more than the other. He enjoys both games because both are equally important to him for different reasons. He likes cricket because he learned it when he was growing up in India. He has lots of memories of playing it with his family, which makes the sport very special to him. However, baseball is also important to him because it was the first sport he learned with his new friends in America. For him, it is associated with the start of a whole new life, so it is also very special to him.

The author thinks of America as his other homeland because he has grown to be comfortable and "at home" here. He has found a lot of friends and he enjoys playing sports with them. He started a while new life when he came here and embarrassed the American culture. He feels a special connection to both places.

The narrator feels lucky because he has a bond with two places. He has good memories of living in India and playing cricket with his family. However, he also has a really good life and future here in the United States. He can see that he is lucky to be where he is and to have friends and family who love him. The narrator is lucky to have learned both of these sports in his homelands.

Related Lumos Online Workbook: Correct Use of Adjectives and Adverbs; Correct Subject-Verb Agreement; Recognize Pronouns; Demonstrate Command of Capitalization; Demonstrate Command of Punctuation; Correct Spelling (CCSS: L.6.1, L.6.2, L.6.3)

Reading Task 3 Answer Key

Question No.	Answer	Related Lumos Online Workbook	CCSS
20	A	Analysis of Key Events and Ideas; Conclusions Drawn from the Text; Development of Ideas; Over-all Development of Ideas; Develop Setting	RL.6.1, RL.6.5
21	B	Use Context Clue to Determine Word Meaning; Use Clues to Determine Multiple-Meaning Words; Use Common Roots and Affixes; Consult Reference Materials	L.6.4
22	D	Analysis of Key Events and Ideas	RL.6.1
23	A	Analysis of Key Events and Ideas	RL.6.1
24	C	Summary of Text; Central Idea of the Text	RI.6.2
25	D	Analysis of Key Events and Ideas; Conclusions Drawn from the Text; Development of Ideas; Over-all Development of Ideas; Develop Setting	RL.6.1, RL.6.5

Question No.	Answer	Related Lumos Online Workbook	CCSS
26	A	Analysis of Key Events and Ideas; Conclusions Drawn from the Text; Development of Ideas; Overall Development of Ideas; Develop Setting	RL.6.1, RL.6.5
27	A	Analysis of Key Events and Ideas; Conclusions Drawn from the Text; Development of Ideas; Summary of Text	RL.6.1, RL.6.2

Sample Answer for Open–Ended Question 3

A 4-point response should include:
- Answer to all parts of the question
- Reference to the text in response
- Personal comparisons

My schedule is very structured, just like the poet's schedule is. I get up at the same time each day to catch the bus for school. Then, I have class all day and after school I go to dance class, have dinner and after that I do homework at night. It is always a full day. There is not usually much time to daydream or rest because I am so busy.

Even though our schedules are similar, I don't have the exact same classes or activities as the poet. I don't take Latin or piano lessons, although I am thinking of starting to learn how to play guitar. Right now, my school doesn't offer Latin. My parents are looking for a place where I can learn Spanish. I can relate to what the poet is going through because sometimes I wish I had some free time so I could rest.

If I had more free time I would like to start painting. I have always wanted to try it. I think it would be very relaxing and would also be a great way to decorate my room. I think my parents would be willing to let me try if it wasn't so expensive!

Related Lumos Online Workbook: Correct Use of Adjectives and Adverbs; Correct Subject-Verb Agreement; Recognize Pronouns; Demonstrate Command of Capitalization; Demonstrate Command of Punctuation; Correct Spelling (CCSS: L.6.1, L.6.2, L.6.3)

Reading Task 4 Answer Key

Question No.	Answer	Related Lumos Online Workbook	CCSS
29	B	Structure of Text; Central Idea of the Text	RI.6.5
30	B	Analysis of Key Events and Ideas; Conclusions Drawn from the Text	RI.6.1
31	C	Analysis of Key Events and Ideas; Conclusions Drawn from the Text	RI.6.1
32	B	Analysis of Key Events and Ideas; Conclusions Drawn from the Text	RI.6.1

LumosLearning.com

Question No.	Answer	Related Lumos Online Workbook	CCSS
33	D	Use Context Clue to Determine Word Meaning; Use Clues to Determine Multiple-Meaning Words; Use Common Roots and Affixes; Consult Reference Materials	L.6.4
34	D	Analysis of Key Events and Ideas; Conclusions Drawn from the Text	RI.6.1
35	B	Analysis of Key Events and Ideas; Conclusions Drawn from the Text; Structure of Text; Central Idea of the Text	RI.6.1, RI.6.5
36	A	Use Context Clue to Determine Word Meaning; Use Clues to Determind Multiple-Meaning Words; Use Common Roots and Affixes; Consult Reference Materials	L.6.4
37	C	Analysis of Key Events and Ideas; Conclusions Drawn from the Text	RI.6.1

Sample Answer for Open–Ended Question 4

A 4-point response should include:

- Answer to all parts of the question
- Reference to the text in response
- Personal comparisons

I am not sure I consider leeches to be "heroes," but they are helpful. I understand that they are valuable and have helped save human lives. However, I have always been taught that heroes are brave and risk things to help others like soldiers, police officers, or fire fighters. I am not sure the leeches are making a choice to help humans. Mostly humans are using them to help themselves.

If leeches became extinct, the medical community would need to find other options for blood-letting. Personally, I have never seen any leeches when I went to the doctors, so I am not sure how many people would be impacted by their loss. Maybe in other countries they play a bigger role than they do in the United States.

In the future I think leeches will be used more for research than to treat patients. Doctors will try to understand how their saliva and the chemicals inside them can be used to help people who are sick. It is clear that leeches have some positive qualities, but people are more likely to be open to using leeches in this way than in putting them on their bodies.

Related Lumos Online Workbook: Correct Use of Adjectives and Adverbs; Correct Subject-Verb Agreement; Recognize Pronouns; Demonstrate Command of Capitalization; Demonstrate Command of Punctuation; Correct Spelling (CCSS: L.6.1, L.6.2, L.6.3)

Notes

LumosLearning.com

Practice Test - 1

Student Name:

Test Date:

Start Time:

End Time:

Writing Task 1

Here are some reminders for when you are completing this Writing Task:

- Using the situation given below as a guide, write a story in your own words.
- You may take notes, create a web, or do other prewriting work. Then, write your story on a sheet of paper.
- After you complete writing your composition, read whatever you have written. Make sure that your writing is the best it can be.

Writing Situation: You went to spend a day at the beach recently. You were very disappointed to see how much the beach was polluted. People were leaving their garbage everywhere. There were half eaten food, empty bottles, cans and plastic bags all over the place. You decided that you would do something about this mess.

Writing Task: Write an article to the local newspaper about the disappointing mess on the beach. In your article be sure to describe the situation and explain why it is important to keep public places clean and also discuss how the public could help in keeping these places clean.

Prewriting Area

 LumosLearning.com

Writing Task 1

LumosLearning.com

Reading Task 1

Directions to the Student

Now you will read a story and answer the questions that follow.
Some questions will be multiple-choice; others will be open-ended.

- You may look back at the reading passage as often as you want.
- Read each question carefully and think about the answer and completely fill in the circle next to your choice.
- If you do not know the answer to a question, go on to the next question and come back to the skipped question later.

My BFF

Staring intently into each other's eyes, Megan and I pledged: "We are friends...through thick and thin...through the ups and the downs...you are my BFF...my best friend forever."

That was two years ago, when Megan and I were in the fourth grade and things were different. Life wasn't complicated. We lived next door to each other and did everything together. We were inseparable. My pesky older brother even nicknamed us "the Siamese Twins."

Now, Megan and I are in middle school. Megan likes to hang out at the skate park while I like to hang out at the mall. Megan isn't doing well in some of her classes and I have a few honor classes. I love hip hop music and Megan is into punk rock. And the worst thing of all is that life suddenly got complicated. Megan's mom and dad divorced last summer so now Megan spends every weekend across town with her dad. Now, we hardly ever spend any time together. We're definitely not "the Siamese Twins" any more.

"Hey, Jas did you hear me?"

"Oh, sorry Mom, what did you say?"

My mom sighed. "You seem lost in your thoughts," she says. "What's wrong?"

"Oh nothing...Well, just thinking about Megan," I moan.

"Hmmm, let me guess," Mom replies. "You're wondering why the two of you aren't as close as you used to be, right?"

"Gee Mom, what are you...the Amazing Kreskin? How did you know what I was thinking?"

Mom chuckles, "Oh Jasmine, I'm your mother. Listen," she said more seriously, "change is part of growing-up. You and Megan are growing-up and you have different interests now. Plus, she adds, "You know that things are tough for Megan. Her parents just got divorced and she has to adjust to the new living situation."

"Mom, you're sort of right," I replied while thinking of my BFF pledge with Megan. "Just because we have different interests doesn't mean that our friendship has to dissolve. I know she's having a difficult time dealing with her parents' divorce. Why can't she just talk to me? She used to tell me everything," I whined.

Mom sat quietly for a few minutes and then her face lit up like a beam of light. "Listen, I have an idea," she said. "Why don't you think of something fun that you and Megan enjoyed doing together and try recreating it? You know, like a blast from the past…the good old days."

Suddenly, ideas start racing through my mind like a swarm of excited bees. I gave Mom a big kiss on the cheek and said, "Thanks!" as I jumped off the sofa and ran upstairs to my room.

Lying in bed that night, I came up with a plan so amazing I could hardly sleep. In the morning, I sent Megan a text message: M- meet me @ the spot 2day @ 4 –J.

After school, I rushed home, changed my clothes and grabbed my bag of surprises. I didn't want to be late meeting Megan.

"Wassup, Jas? Why did you wanna meet here?" Megan asked with one eyebrow raised.

I smiled. "Sprinkles, chocolate syrup, or both? This is my treat."

She smiled. "Uh, both of course."

"Great, grab a table while I get the sundae," I said, "And here, go through this," I continued as I handed Megan a large manila envelope.

"Hey, do you want me to take that big bag you're carrying," Megan asked.

"No, I got it. I'll be there in a minute."

As I looked over at the table, I could see Megan open the envelope. She looked surprised to see the contents. There were about two dozen pictures, and not just any pictures. They were all pictures from every holiday we had spent together over the years. The Halloween when I was Thing 1 and she dressed up as Thing 2. The Christmas when I bought each of us a matching sweater and scarf set to wear with our skinny jeans. There were even pictures from the 4th of July barbecue when we had eaten way too much egg salad and couldn't stop passing gas.

"Hey, where did you find all these old pics?" Megan asked me after I sat down at the table.

"I went through the photo album we put together last summer," I replied as I handed Megan a spoon.

"Mmmm, this sundae is so good," said Megan, "I haven't had one of these since…" her voice trailed off. "Since the day we made our pledge."

"Meg, I know things aren't the same, but I wanted to do something to remind us of the good times we used to have together. Your friendship still means a lot to me and I want you to know that I'm still here for you."

Megan gazed out of the window and then turned and said, "Well, um…I am having some trouble with my math class. Do you think you can help me out?"

"Sure, I can. But can you do me a favor and teach me how to use one of these?" I reached down, opened the big bag I had been carrying and pulled out a hot pink skateboard.

Megan started laughing and said, "Totally… I can't wait to help out my BFF!"

LumosLearning.com

1. Why were the girls described as "staring intently" in the opening statement of the passage?

   Ⓐ The mood was humorous.
   Ⓑ The mood was important.
   Ⓒ The mood was painful.
   Ⓓ The mood was loving.

2. In the second paragraph, which word helps the reader figure out the meaning of the nickname, "the Siamese Twins"?

   Ⓐ pesky
   Ⓑ inseparable
   Ⓒ complicated
   Ⓓ different

3. What is a synonym for "pesky"?

   Ⓐ annoying
   Ⓑ irritating
   Ⓒ horrible
   Ⓓ all of these

4. Which reason would best explain why Megan isn't doing well in some of her classes?

   Ⓐ She hates school.
   Ⓑ She spends too much time at the skate park.
   Ⓒ She is struggling with her parents' divorce and this is probably affecting her school work.
   Ⓓ She's trying to make new friends and doesn't want to appear too smart.

5. What kind of occupation would the Amazing Kreskin most likely have?

   Ⓐ magician
   Ⓑ computer programmer
   Ⓒ mind reader
   Ⓓ actor

6. How does the reader know that Jasmine took her mother's advice?

   Ⓐ Jasmine asked Megan to meet her at their favorite ice cream parlor.
   Ⓑ Jasmine shared memorable photos with Megan.
   Ⓒ Jasmine told Megan that she wanted to do something to remind them of the good times they used to have together.
   Ⓓ All of these

7. The author most likely wrote this story to

    Ⓐ inform the reader
    Ⓑ persuade the reader
    Ⓒ anger the reader
    Ⓓ entertain the reader

8. What type of writing is this passage?

    Ⓐ nonfiction
    Ⓑ fiction
    Ⓒ science fiction
    Ⓓ poetry

9. Which statement would not explain why Jasmine asked Megan to teach her how to skateboard?

    Ⓐ Jasmine wanted to show Megan that she was interested in learning how to do something that Megan enjoyed.
    Ⓑ Jasmine wanted to prove that she could be better at skateboarding than Megan.
    Ⓒ Jasmine admired the fact that Megan could skateboard.
    Ⓓ Jasmine wanted to spend more time with Megan.

Open-Ended Question 1

Here are some reminders for when you are completing this Open-Ended Question:

- Read the passage "My BFF" and the open-ended question and write your answer on a sheet of paper.
- Focus your response on the question asked.
- Answer all parts of the question and explain your answer with specific details.
- Use specific information from the story to answer all the parts of the question.

10. The passage describes a challenging situation between two best friends.

- **Discuss how the challenge between the friends was resolved.**
- **Describe how you think Jasmine's mother was helpful with resolving the situation.**
- **Explain whether or not you think Jasmine and Megan will remain best friends forever.**

LumosLearning.com

Writing Task 2

Here are some reminders for when you are completing this Writing Task:

- Using the situation given below as a guide, write a story in your own words.
- You may take notes, create a web, or do other prewriting work. Then, write your story on a sheet of paper.
- After you complete writing your composition, read whatever you have written. Make sure that your writing is the best it can be.

Writing Situation: Choose a vivid moment, day or time from your childhood. For example you might think of the first time that you rode a school bus, earned money to buy something that you really wanted, the first time you ever learned how to skate or ride a bike, or some other event that stands out in your childhood.

Writing Task: Narrate the events related to the childhood memory you've chosen in such a way that your readers will understand why that particular memory is so important and memorable to you.

Prewriting Area

Writing Task 2

LumosLearning.com

LumosLearning.com

Reading Task 2

Directions to the Student

Now you will read another passage and answer the questions that follow. Some questions will be multiple-choice; others will be open-ended.

- You may look back at the reading passage as often as you want.
- Read each question carefully and think about the answer and completely fill in the circle next to your choice.
- If you do not know the answer to a question, go on to the next question and come back to the skipped question later.

Which world does the future hold for thee?
By Kia Simmons

Abracadabra said the magician
1-2-3
Now close your eyes.
What do you see?
I see
A world filled with color
A world filled with light
A world filled with possibilities
This world is such a magnificent sight!
Abracadabra said the magician
1-2-3
Now close your eyes.
What do you see?
I see
A world filled with despair
A world filled with doom
A world filled with chaos
This world is such a vision of gloom!
Abracadabra said the magician
1-2-3
Now close your eyes.
Which world does the future hold for thee?

11. What is the genre of the above passage?

Ⓐ nonfiction
Ⓑ realistic fiction
Ⓒ poetry
Ⓓ reference

12. What is the main idea of the above poem?

Ⓐ It describes the world you want to see.
Ⓑ It describes the magicians' world.
Ⓒ It describes two kinds of worlds.
Ⓓ It describes the worlds and wants you to choose your future world.

13. What happened when the author closed her eyes the first time?

Ⓐ The author saw a world filled with sorrow.
Ⓑ The author saw a beautiful world.
Ⓒ The author did not see anything.
Ⓓ The author fell asleep.

14. Read the following stanza:

"I see
A world filled with color
A world filled with light
A world filled with possibilities
This world is such a magnificent sight!"

What might be the author's mood when she is seeing this kind of a world?

Ⓐ Very excited
Ⓑ Very upset
Ⓒ Very sad
Ⓓ Very relaxed

15. How does the author feel about the world when she is disappointed?

Ⓐ Magnificent
Ⓑ Lively
Ⓒ Gloomy
Ⓓ Abracadabra

16. Which of the following words is a synonym for "despair"?

Ⓐ democracy
Ⓑ desire
Ⓒ cheerful
Ⓓ misery

17. "A world filled with possibilities"

Read the above line. What is the meaning of the word "possibilities"?

Ⓐ chances
Ⓑ prospects
Ⓒ odds
Ⓓ many things that are possible

18. What did the author see when she closed her eyes for the second time?

Ⓐ a world filled with chaos and gloom
Ⓑ a world filled with joy and color
Ⓒ a world filled with both joy and chaos
Ⓓ a world filled with neither joy nor chaos

19. This world is such a magnificent sight!

What is the adjective in the above sentence?

Ⓐ sight
Ⓑ magnificent
Ⓒ world
Ⓓ such

Open-Ended Question 2

Here are some reminders for when you are completing this Open-Ended Question:

- Read the passage "Which world does the future hold for thee?" and the open-ended question and write your answer on a sheet of paper.
- Focus your response on the question asked.
- Answer all parts of the question and explain your answer with specific details.
- Use specific information from the story to answer all the parts of the question.

20. After reading the above poem:

- Discuss the summary of the poem.
- Describe the difference in the mood of the author when she sees the first and the second worlds.
- Explain which of the worlds you would like to see and why.

Reading Task 3

Directions to the Student

Now you will read a story and answer the questions that follow.
Some questions will be multiple-choice; others will be open-ended.

- You may look back at the reading passage as often as you want.
- Read each question carefully and think about the answer and completely fill in the circle next to your choice.
- If you do not know the answer to a question, go on to the next question and come back to the skipped question later.

Letters to My Soldier Dad

February 10, 2005

Hey Dad,

How are you doing? Mom is still bummed that you were deployed to Iraq two weeks before Isabel's first birthday, but she knows that you are risking your life for our country and she's really proud of you (so am I). Speaking of birthdays, I overheard Mom talking to Aunt Carmen about Cousin Maria's Quinceañera celebration. I think they want me to be in the Quinceañera Court, but I don't want to dress up in a tuxedo and look like a penguin. Anyway, I know I won't have a choice in the matter so complaining is a waste of time. I'm working on a new model plane, the Vought F4U-1A Corsair. It's a classic! I can't wait to finish assembling it so I can send you some pictures.

Stay Safe!
Te quiero, Miguel
AKA Your Little Soldier

March 25, 2005

Hi Dad,

Did you get the pictures of the plane? Could you see the plane's glazed canopy...awesome, right??

I'm saving up money to buy the Schleicher ASK 21 Glider. The kit is on sale for $25 — 30% percent off the regular price — that's a great deal. Oh, we started rehearsing for Maria's Quinceañera. I'm actually having a good time. The girl I'm escorting is really cute. Maria is having a fairytale princess theme. I know it sounds kind of girly but it's actually pretty cool. We're going to do a hip hop dance and a famous rapper is supposed to perform. Maria won't tell anyone who the mystery rapper is, so rumors are going around the school about who the rapper might be.

LumosLearning.com

People keep coming up to me asking me if I know who is getting invited to the party. I feel like a famous celebrity.

Stay Safe!
Te quiero, Miguel
AKA Your Little Soldier

April 5, 2005

Hey Dad!
Guess what? Isabel just started walking! Wait, Mom probably already told you this. Anyway, Izzy looks so funny when she's trying to keep her balance. I missed the sale, but Mom got the plane for me at the regular price because she thought I did a great job in Maria's Quinceañera. Actually, it turned out to be an awesome experience and I got a new girlfriend out of it. Her name is Carmen. Can you believe that Maria got Daddy Yankee to perform at her 15th birthday party? Maria entered womanhood in style! I wish you could've been there.

Stay Safe!
Te quiero, Miguel
AKA Your Little Soldier

P.S. I broke the wing off of your beloved P-51D Mustang IV Fighter. Gotcha! Okay, you can pick yourself up off the floor now. Hope you enjoyed my belated April fool's joke!

21. This passage is

  Ⓐ a group of letters
  Ⓑ fiction
  Ⓒ poetry
  Ⓓ biography

22. The overall tone of the passage is

  Ⓐ depressing
  Ⓑ angry
  Ⓒ optimistic
  Ⓓ sarcastic

23. Based on the passage, the reader knows that Miguel's family is

  Ⓐ Japanese
  Ⓑ Hispanic
  Ⓒ Russian
  Ⓓ Italian

24. What part of the passage informs the reader that Miguel's Dad also has a collection of model airplanes?

  Ⓐ The Feb. 10th letter
  Ⓑ The March 25th letter
  Ⓒ The April 5th letter
  Ⓓ The first letter

25. Which statement would not be a reason that the author included information about Miguel wanting to buy the model airplane on sale?

  Ⓐ Miguel's family tries to save money.
  Ⓑ Buying model airplane kits can be expensive.
  Ⓒ Miguel's family is rich.
  Ⓓ Miguel knows that his father would want the family to watch their budget.

26. The word, "bummed", is slang for:

  Ⓐ happy
  Ⓑ disappointed
  Ⓒ excited
  Ⓓ relieved

LumosLearning.com

27. Which word informs the reader that Miguel's Dad is an active soldier in the Iraq War?

    Ⓐ Quinceañera
    Ⓑ canopy
    Ⓒ deployed
    Ⓓ assembling

28. A Quinceañera is

    Ⓐ similar to a Sweet 16 celebration
    Ⓑ the Hispanic tradition of celebrating a girl's 15th birthday
    Ⓒ a celebration of a young girl's coming of age
    Ⓓ all of these

29. How does the reader know that Carmen is probably the girl Miguel escorted in the Quinceañera?

    Ⓐ Miguel told his father that girl he is escorting is really cute.
    Ⓑ Miguel said he got a girlfriend from participating in the Quinceañera.
    Ⓒ Neither "A" nor "B"
    Ⓓ Both "A" and "B"

Open-Ended Question 3

Here are some reminders for when you are completing this Open-Ended Question: • Read the passage "Letters to My Soldier Dad" and the open-ended question and write your answer on a sheet of paper. • Focus your response on the question asked. • Answer all parts of the question and explain your answer with specific details. • Use specific information from the story to answer all the parts of the question.

30. In the passage "Letters to My Soldier Dad", Miguel sends letters to his father who is a soldier in Iraq.

   • Describe why you think it is important for Miguel to write often to his father.
   • Discuss why you think Miguel closes each letter in the same way.
   • Explain what you think Miguel will probably write about in his next letter to his father.

LumosLearning.com

Reading Task 4

Directions to the Student

Now you will read a story and answer the questions that follow.
Some questions will be multiple-choice; others will be open-ended.

- You may look back at the reading passage as often as you want.
- Read each question carefully and think about the answer and completely fill in the circle next to your choice.
- If you do not know the answer to a question, go on to the next question and come back to the skipped question later.

Pets Are Good for Your Health

Would you be surprised if your doctor writes you a prescription that tells you to get a pet? Well, don't be surprised. Today, a growing number of medical experts are doing just that because they are starting to realize that pills and other medications aren't always the best cure for an illness.

Many medical experts have reported that pets are good for your heart. Several studies have found that people who have had a heart attack survive longer with a pet than without. For example, in a study of 6,000 people conducted by the Baker Medical Research Institute in Australia, researchers found that those who kept pets had lower blood pressures and lower cholesterol levels which also meant a lower risk of heart attack. Other medical studies have found that people who owned a cat or dog were able to handle stressful situations better than those without these pets.

Also, many medical studies have shown that having a pet can keep you from feeling lonely and depressed because pets can help you relax and focus your attention away from your problems and worries. Some people enjoy watching fish swim in an aquarium because it can be very soothing while other people find a visit to the zoo helps them relieve stress.

Have you ever come home from a tough day at school and just hearing the bark of your dog or purr of your cat made you feel better? One five-year study of 600 children aged 3-18 found that children with pets who may be struggling in school, or whose parents had divorced, had higher levels of self-esteem than those without a pet.

So which kind of pet provides the most health benefits? Usually, dogs and cats are mentioned in medical studies. However, any animal has the potential to improve your health and brighten your day.

31. According to the passage, why are doctors prescribing pets to help patients cure illnesses?

Ⓐ Pets are cheaper than buying pills or other forms of medication.
Ⓑ Insurance companies are forcing doctors to write prescriptions for pets.
Ⓒ Pills and other medications are not always the best cure for an illness.
Ⓓ Pets can cure any illness.

32. Pets have helped

Ⓐ People who are stressed
Ⓑ People lower their blood pressure
Ⓒ People who have had heart attacks
Ⓓ All of these

33. A person with high blood pressure is at greater risk of

Ⓐ Having a heart attack
Ⓑ Not dealing with stress well
Ⓒ Needing more than one pet
Ⓓ Needing fish only

34. What is an antonym for "depression"?

Ⓐ Sadness
Ⓑ Despair
Ⓒ Misery
Ⓓ Happiness

35. What is a synonym for soothing?

Ⓐ Laughing
Ⓑ Agitated
Ⓒ Irritating
Ⓓ Calming

36. Based on the passage, which statement is not true?

Ⓐ Pets have helped children deal with stress.
Ⓑ Pets have helped children struggling with school.
Ⓒ Pets have helped children of divorce.
Ⓓ Pets have helped destroy children's self-esteem.

37. This passage is

    Ⓐ Fiction
    Ⓑ Realistic fiction
    Ⓒ Nonfiction
    Ⓓ Poetry

38. Which statement is not a reason for having pets?

    Ⓐ Pets are a distraction from problems and worries.
    Ⓑ Pets cause more stress.
    Ⓒ Pets help improve a person's mood.
    Ⓓ Pets can be soothing.

39. Based on the passage, which animal has the most health benefits?

    Ⓐ Cats
    Ⓑ Dogs
    Ⓒ Cats & Dogs
    Ⓓ Any animal

Open-Ended Question 4

40. The passage describes the health benefits of having a pet.

- Describe a situation where a doctor might write a patient a prescription for a pet.
- Discuss why you think most of the medical studies about having a pet mention dogs and cats.
- Explain what kind of pet you would get if your doctor wanted you to get a pet.

End Of Practice Test - 1

LumosLearning.com

Practice Test 1 Answers

Sample Answer for Writing Task 1

A 5-point response should include

- Answers to all parts of the question
- Reference to the text in the response
- Personal comparisons

Dear Editor,

This past weekend I went to the beach with my family. We were upset to find that it was covered in garbage. We couldn't believe that our community would leave it so messy. We were disappointed by what we saw.

I wanted to write you this letter so that I could make a request to the public to take more pride in our natural resources. Our beach is one of the best things our community has. It gives us a safe and fun place to play and spend time with our families. Best of all it is free. It doesn't cost anything to sit by the waves and enjoy time with friends.

The beach will only be a resource as long as we take care of it. If we cover it with garbage, no one will want to visit it any more. Stray animals and bugs will start taking the beach over because of all the free food lying around. Fish and wildlife could die because of all the pollution that is thrown into the water.

In school we learn that we have to take care of the environment, and that includes the beautiful beaches in our community. The beach gives us all a lot of enjoyment. It is our responsibility to take care of it.

Thank you for listening.

Sincerely,
Jackie Johnson
Grade 6

Related Lumos Online Workbook: Correct Use of Adjectives and Adverbs; Correct Subject-Verb Agreement; Recognize Pronouns; Demonstrate Command of Capitalization; Demonstrate Command of Punctuation; Correct Spelling (CCSS: L.6.1, L.6.2, L.6.3)

Reading Task 1 Answer Key

Question No.	Answer	Related Lumos Online Workbook	CCSS
1	B	Figurative Words and Phrases; Connotative Words and Phrases	RL.6.4
2	B	Use Context Clue to Determind Word Meaning; Use Clues to Determind Multiple-Meaning Words; Use Common Roots and Affixes; Consult Reference Materials	L.6.4
3	D	Figurative Words and Phrases; Connotative Words and Phrases	RL.6.4
4	C	Analysis of Key Events and Ideas; Conclusions Drawn from the Text;	RL.6.1
5	C	Use Context Clue to Determind Word Meaning; Use Clues to Determind Multiple-Meaning Words; Use Common Roots and Affixes; Consult Reference Materials	L.6.4
6	D	Analysis of Key Events and Ideas; Conclusions Drawn from the Text;	RL.6.1
7	D	Development of Ideas; Summary of Text	RL.6.2
8	B	Analysis of Key Events and Ideas; Conclusions Drawn from the Text;	RL.6.1
9	B	Development of Ideas; Develop Setting	RL.6.5

Sample Answer for Open–Ended Question 1

A 4-point response should include:
- Answer to all parts of the question
- Reference to the text in response
- Personal comparisons

Jasmine resolved the challenging situation between her and her best friend. The challenging situation that Jasmine encountered was that she was growing apart from her best friend. Jasmine wanted to resolve the situation, so she planned a special activity that would remind her friend of the times they used to spend together, and took an interest in Megan's new hobby, skateboarding, so they could have a more current connection together.

Jasmine's mom was helpful in getting the two friends back together. Since Jasmine was sad and didn't know what to do about her friend growing so far apart, her mom suggested a blast from the past. Jasmine sprang into action and her head was full of ideas for bringing she and her friend back together.

I am not sure if Jasmine and Megan will remain best friends forever. Life can change very quickly, especially when you grow up. If they both make an effort to understand each other and be there for each other, it is definitely possible. My mom is still friends with some of the people she went to elementary school with. They aren't best friends because they don't see each other as often as they used to, but they do enjoy catching up and I know they will care about each other forever.

Related Lumos Online Workbook: Correct Use of Adjectives and Adverbs; Correct Subject-Verb Agreement; Recognize Pronouns; Demonstrate Command of Capitalization; Demonstrate Command of Punctuation; Correct Spelling (CCSS: L.6.1, L.6.2, L.6.3)

Sample Answer for Writing Task 2

A 5-point response should include
- Answers to all parts of the question
- Reference to the text in the response
- Personal comparisons

There are many great moments that stand out from my childhood memories. The one moment that stands out most from my childhood is that my grandparents lived nearby. From the time I was a baby, our family visited them at least once a month.

When I was in third grade, my grandfather invited me to stay overnight on our next visit. My parents agreed, and I was really excited. I got to spend the whole night with my grandparents and have a sleepover. I was sure they were going to let me stay up past my bedtime.

The next weekend, we visited on a Saturday and my parents left me there in the afternoon. I helped my grandfather in his garden. We shoveled soil into this machine he had that ground it into very fine particles, which we then scattered in the garden. We also picked tomatoes and peppers. Then, my grandmother cooked a great dinner using the tomatoes and peppers we picked, and she also made her famous oatmeal bread.

After dinner, my grandfather showed me photographs and told me stories about working as a teenager in a shipyard that built sailing ships, and about his job as an agent for the owner of a fleet of sailing ships when he was an adult. His stories were interesting; the days of large sailing ships carrying cargo around the world are gone now. Therefore, he gave me a glimpse into history and I learned a lot. I will never forget the first weekend I spent with my grandparents. Having my grandparents live nearby allowed me to have many fantastic memories with them during my childhood.

Related Lumos Online Workbook: Correct Use of Adjectives and Adverbs; Correct Subject-Verb Agreement; Recognize Pronouns; Demonstrate Command of Capitalization; Demonstrate Command of Punctuation; Correct Spelling (CCSS: L.6.1, L.6.2, L.6.3)

Reading Task 2 Answer Key

Question No.	Answer	Related Lumos Online Workbook	CCSS
11	C	Analysis of Key Events and Ideas; Conclusions Drawn from the Text	RL.6.1
12	D	Development of Ideas; Summary of Text	RL.6.2
13	B	Analysis of Key Events and Ideas; Conclusions Drawn from the Text	RL.6.1
14	A	Figurative Words and Phrases; Connotative Words and Phrases	RL.6.4
15	C	Analysis of Key Events and Ideas; Conclusions Drawn from the Text	RL.6.1, RL.6.5
16	D	Use Context Clue to Determind Word Meaning; Use Clues to Determind Multiple-Meaning Words; Use Common Roots and Affixes; Consult Reference Materials	L.6.4
17	D	Figurative Words and Phrases; Connotative Words and Phrases	RL.6.4

Question No.	Answer	Related Lumos Online Workbook	CCSS
18	A	Analysis of Key Events and Ideas; Conclusions Drawn from the Text;	RL.6.1
19	B	Use Context Clue to Determind Word Meaning; Use Clues to Determind Multiple-Meaning Words; Use Common Roots and Affixes; Consult Reference Materials	L.6.4

Sample Answer for Open-Ended Question 2

A 4-point response should include:
- Answers to all parts of the question
- Reference to the text in the response
- Personal comparisons

The poem talks about two different kinds of worlds. One of the worlds is full of light and possibility, and the other one is full of doom and despair. When the author sees the first one, she is excited by what she sees and all the possibilities there could be. When she sees the second one, she seems frightened and sad. It seems like she would like to run or change what she is seeing very quickly because it is depressing.

Of course I would like to see the first world instead of the second world. The first world is a world of hope and happiness. Who wouldn't prefer to live in a world of joy than one of sadness and negativity? In reality, I think we choose which world we tend to see in our own lives. There are positives and negatives all around us, but it is up to us which lens we use to see the world.

Related Lumos Online Workbook: Correct Use of Adjectives and Adverbs; Correct Subject-Verb Agreement; Recognize Pronouns; Demonstrate Command of Capitalization; Demonstrate Command of Punctuation; Correct Spelling (CCSS: L.6.1, L.6.2, L.6.3)

Reading Task 3 Answer Key

Question No.	Answer	Related Lumos Online Workbook	CCSS
21	A	Analysis of Key Events and Ideas; Conclusions Drawn from the Text	RI.6.1
22	C	Central Idea of the Text; Summary of Text	RI.6.2
23	B	Analysis of Key Events and Ideas; Conclusions Drawn from the Text	RI.6.1
24	C	Analysis of Key Events and Ideas; Conclusions Drawn from the Text	RI.6.1
25	C	Analysis of Key Events and Ideas; Conclusions Drawn from the Text	RI.6.1
26	B	Determine Technical Meanings; Figurative Words and Phrases; Connotative Words and Phrases	RI.6.4
27	C	Determine Technical Meanings; Figurative Words and Phrases; Connotative Words and Phrases	RI.6.4
28	D	Determine Technical Meanings; Figurative Words and Phrases; Connotative Words and Phrases	RI.6.4
29	D	Analysis of Key Events and Ideas; Conclusions Drawn from the Text	RI.6.1

LumosLearning.com

Sample Answer for Open–Ended Question 3

A 4-point response should include:

- Answer to all parts of the question
- Reference to the text in response
- Personal comparisons

Miguel writes to his father so often because he misses him and wants to make sure he keeps him involved in his daily life even though he is fighting for our country overseas. You can tell that he and his father must have been very close because Miguel talks to him about things like girls and family, and lots of boys probably wouldn't do that.

Miguel's father called him Little Soldier, so he closes the letter that way each time so his dad knows he likes being called that and how much his dad means to him even though he is away. He also probably uses the name to feel a connection to his dad.

In his next letter, Miguel will probably tell his dad about the work he has done on his new glider kit. He seems pretty proud of his planes. It must have been something he used to do with his dad when he was home. He will probably also mention his little sister and other things she is learning to do. It is almost like Miguel is being the man of the house by reporting on those types of things and helping his dad stay connected.

Related Lumos Online Workbook: Correct Use of Adjectives and Adverbs; Correct Subject-Verb Agreement; Recognize Pronouns; Demonstrate Command of Capitalization; Demonstrate Command of Punctuation; Correct Spelling (CCSS: L.6.1, L.6.2, L.6.3)

Reading Task 4 Answer Key

Question No.	Answer	Related Lumos Online Workbook	CCSS
31	C	Analysis of Key Events and Ideas; Conclusions Drawn from the Text	RI.6.1
32	D	Analysis of Key Events and Ideas; Conclusions Drawn from the Text; Central Idea of the Text; Summary of Text	RI.6.1, RI.6.2
33	A	Analysis of Key Events and Ideas; Summary of Text; Central Idea of the Text	RI.6.3
34	D	Determine Technical Meanings; Figurative Words and Phrases; Connotative Words and Phrases	RI.6.4
35	D	Determine Technical Meanings; Figurative Words and Phrases; Connotative Words and Phrases	RI.6.4
36	D	Analysis of Key Events and Ideas; Conclusions Drawn from the Text	RI.6.1
37	C	Analysis of Key Events and Ideas; Conclusions Drawn from the Text	RI.6.1
38	B	Analysis of Key Events and Ideas; Conclusions Drawn from the Text	RI.6.1
39	D	Analysis of Key Events and Ideas; Conclusions Drawn from the Text	RI.6.1

Sample Answer for Open–Ended Question 4

CCSS: L6.1, L6.2, L6.3

A 4-point response should include:

- Answers to all parts of the question
- Reference to the text in response
- Personal comparisons

A doctor might write a prescription to get a pet for someone who had a heart attack or other heart problems because pets seem to help people lower their blood pressure which makes them live longer. I have not personally heard of a doctor writing a prescription for a pet, but I definitely think pets can keep you healthy. Plus, they are a lot more natural than chemicals used in prescription medication.

Most studies probably focus on cats and dogs because they are the most common pets in the United States. They are also the most social and cuddly. They probably have more benefits than fish or snakes or other animals you can't easily hold and play with.

If my doctor told me to get a pet, I would choose a dog. I have always wanted one, and I have never been allowed to get one because my parents think they are too much work to take care of. If I had a doctor's note, they wouldn't have a choice, and they would have to let me get one.

Related Lumos Online Workbook: Correct Use of Adjectives and Adverbs; Correct Subject-Verb Agreement; Recognize Pronouns; Demonstrate Command of Capitalization; Demonstrate Command of Punctuation; Correct Spelling (CCSS: L.6.1, L.6.2, L.6.3)

Notes

Practice Test - 2

Student Name:

Test Date:

Start Time:

End Time:

Writing Task 1

Here are some reminders for when you are completing this Writing Task:

- Using the situation given below as a guide, write a story in your own words.
- You may take notes, create a web, or do other prewriting work. Then, write your story on a sheet of paper.
- After you complete writing your composition, read whatever you have written. Make sure that your writing is the best it can be.

Writing Situation: Most people have had a day that stands out in their minds. It might have been a day when they went somewhere special or something memorable happened. Think about a day that stands out in your memory. Remember who was there and how you felt.

Writing Task: Write an essay explaining what made this day memorable. Support your writing with examples and details. Make sure that your essay has an introduction and a conclusion.

Prewriting Area

Writing Task 1

LumosLearning.com

Reading Task 1

Directions to the Student

Now you will read a story and answer the questions that follow.
Some questions will be multiple-choice; others will be open-ended.

- You may look back at the reading passage as often as you want.
- Read each question carefully and think about the answer and fill in the circle completely next to your choice.
- If you do not know the answer to a question, go on to the next question and come back to the skipped question later.

Poppa P's Personal Blog

My name is Peter Popadora, but everyone calls me Poppa P. I have made a name for myself in the Maple Hills Community. Well, I guess one might even refer to me as a local celebrity. I won the lead role in my school's Winter Musical. I also have a news segment, "News with Poppa P, That's Me!" during the children's hour on our town's radio station. I sing, act, and write movie scripts. When I grow up, I want to be a big time film director and producer – the next Steven Spielberg. However, in the meantime, I will continue to develop my reputation in the Maple Hills community, and I will probably try out for the reality television show, American Star. I really don't want to be the next American Star, but I know it would be the perfect platform to showcase my natural singing ability.

Now, I know what you're probably thinking - this guy sounds very conceited - because I've been called conceited in the past. However, you're wrong! I would not consider myself an arrogant person. Rather, I simply believe in letting the facts about me speak for themselves—just ask anyone.

Well, don't ask anyone at my school or even in my town because they are all haters. They are all jealous of me, the Great Poppa P. It's best if you speak with more neutral parties such as my mom, dad, and Aunt Patty. Even my amateurish little sister, Paula, wouldn't qualify as a reliable reference for me.

Paula claims she also has talent. She thinks she can sing and dance or something. I'm not exactly sure. Anyway, Paula went out of her way to slander me. She recently wrote an article in our school newspaper entitled, "Just Ask Me If You Want to Know the Truth about Poppa P." The article was just a pack of lies. Our dad didn't have to pay my talent agent an extra fee to represent me and our mom certainly didn't have to "strongly persuade" the producer of the news show at the radio station that he'd better give me my own news segment or else. In fact, nothing Paula said about me in that article was even close to the truth. It took me weeks to repair my damaged reputation, but as the saying goes in show business, "bad press is still press."

LumosLearning.com

Her article only increased the public's awareness of Poppa P.

Wondering what's on Poppa P's Spring Agenda? Well, I'm trying out for my school's Spring Talent Showcase. I haven't decided whether I will sing a love ballad or perform a dramatic soliloquy. Only time will tell. Also, I was thinking about organizing some kind of community event...no, delete that idea.

Until next time,
Poppa P

1. What type of fiction is this passage?

   Ⓐ satire
   Ⓑ poem
   Ⓒ drama
   Ⓓ tragedy

2. In the passage the author

   Ⓐ describes the advantages of being a child entertainer
   Ⓑ describes the disadvantages of being a child entertainer
   Ⓒ exaggerates the personality of a child entertainer
   Ⓓ none of these

3. Based on the passage, Poppa P's biggest fan is:

   Ⓐ Steven Spielberg
   Ⓑ Paula
   Ⓒ Aunt Patty
   Ⓓ himself

4. Poppa P is:

   Ⓐ overly confident
   Ⓑ ordinary
   Ⓒ shy
   Ⓓ sociable

5. An antonym for the word "conceited" is:

   Ⓐ vain
   Ⓑ proud
   Ⓒ arrogant
   Ⓓ humble

6. What does Poppa P mean when he refers to the show, American Star, as the perfect platform to showcase his natural singing ability?

   Ⓐ The show has a raised stage he can stand on.
   Ⓑ The show is a great place to demonstrate his singing voice.
   Ⓒ The show is environmentally friendly.
   Ⓓ The show will pit him against his sister.

LumosLearning.com

7. Which statement tells the reader what the saying "bad press is still press" means?

    Ⓐ It took me weeks to repair my damaged reputation.
    Ⓑ Paula went out of her way to slander me.
    Ⓒ Her article only increased the public's awareness of Poppa P.
    Ⓓ Paula destroyed Poppa P.'s reputation.

8. Based on the passage, the reader would know that a dramatic soliloquy is performed by:

    Ⓐ 1 actor
    Ⓑ 2 actors
    Ⓒ 3 actors
    Ⓓ 4 or more actors

9. Poppa P most likely deleted the idea of organizing a community event because

    Ⓐ It would be too much work for him.
    Ⓑ He is not good at organizing events.
    Ⓒ He prefers to work on solo projects.
    Ⓓ He will need Paula's help.

Open-Ended Question 1

Here are some reminders for when you are completing this Open-Ended Question:
• Read the passage "Poppa P's Personal Blog" and the open-ended question and write your answer on a sheet of paper. • Focus your response on the question asked. • Answer all parts of the question and explain your answer with specific details. • Use specific information from the story to answer all the parts of the question.

10. In the passage, Poppa P reveals that many people, including his own sister, don't like him.

   • Describe why you think people may not like Poppa P.
   • Discuss whether or not you think Poppa P would make a good friend.
   • Explain how you think Poppa P could become more likeable to others.

© Lumos Information Services 2013   LumosLearning.com

LumosLearning.com

Writing Task 2

Here are some reminders for when you are completing this Writing Task:

- Using the situation given below as a guide, write a story in your own words.
- You may take notes, create a web, or do other prewriting work. Then, write your story on a sheet of paper.
- After you complete writing your composition, read whatever you have written. Make sure that your writing is the best it can be.

Writing Situation: Prejudice is defined as an unfavorable opinion or feeling formed beforehand or without knowledge, thought, or reason. Prejudice is often the cause of discriminatory behavior.

Writing Task: Discuss what causes prejudice. Describe the consequences of acting on prejudices. Explain the causes and effects of prejudice.

Prewriting Area

Writing Task 2

Reading Task 2

Directions to the Student

**Now you will read a poem and answer the questions that follow.
Some questions will be multiple-choice; others will be open-ended.**

- You may look back at the reading passage as often as you want.
- Read each question carefully and think about the answer and completely fill in the circle next to your choice.
- If you do not know the answer to a question, go on to the next question and come back to the skipped question later.

A Frenemy

One day
The two of you are best friends
Hanging out watching the game
Or shopping at the mall
Sharing secrets and extra cheesy nachos
The next day
The two of you are worst enemies
Hiding behind those trusting eyes
Was a toxic person green with envy
Eager to make your secrets public knowledge
Friend + Enemy
Always equals
A Frenemy

By Kia Simmons

     LumosLearning.com

11. "Hiding behind those trusting eyes was a toxic person green with envy"

Read the above line. What does the word "toxic" mean?

Ⓐ jealousy
Ⓑ poisonous
Ⓒ poison
Ⓓ conceited

12. Who is a Frenemy?

Ⓐ A friend
Ⓑ an enemy
Ⓒ a relative
Ⓓ a friend who is an enemy

13. According to the above poem what do the two best friends do?

Ⓐ They are eager to make each other's secrets public
Ⓑ They share secrets, extra cheesy nachos or shop at the mall
Ⓒ Both "A" and "B"
Ⓓ None of these

14. What is the above poem about?

Ⓐ friends who could never be enemies
Ⓑ enemies
Ⓒ friends who can also be enemies
Ⓓ best friends

15. What is the genre of the above passage?

Ⓐ Poetry
Ⓑ Drama
Ⓒ Satire
Ⓓ Fiction

16. Which of the following is the best description of a friend?

Ⓐ one you cannot have fun with
Ⓑ one you cannot trust with your secrets
Ⓒ one you can trust with your secrets
Ⓓ one you can never trust

17. What is the main characteristic of an enemy?

   Ⓐ trustworthy
   Ⓑ friendly
   Ⓒ untrustworthy
   Ⓓ helpful

18. Which of the following would be a best definition for Frenemy?

   Ⓐ a friend that is a best friend
   Ⓑ a best friend one day and the worst enemy the next day
   Ⓒ a best friend one day and a good friend the next day
   Ⓓ a person who you can trust always

19. What would be the best synonym for the word "envy"?

   Ⓐ caring
   Ⓑ admire
   Ⓒ jealous
   Ⓓ helpful

LumosLearning.com

Open-Ended Question 2

Here are some reminders for when you are completing this Open-Ended Question:

- Read the passage "A Frenemy" and the open-ended question and write your answer on a sheet of paper.
- Focus your response on the question asked.
- Answer all parts of the question and explain your answer with specific details.
- Use specific information from the story to answer all the parts of the question.

20. The above poem describes friends and enemies. After reading the above poem:

- **Describe a person that is your Frenemy.**
- **Discuss the contrast between best friends and worst enemies.**
- **Explain how you feel about a person who is a Frenemy.**

Reading Task 3

Directions to the Student

Now you will read another passage and answer the questions that follow.
Some questions will be multiple-choice; others will be open-ended.

- You may look back at the reading passage as often as you want.
- Read each question carefully and think about the answer and completely fill in the circle next to your choice.
- If you do not know the answer to a question, go on to the next question and come back to the skipped question later.

The History of the New York City Marathon

Each year, runners from around the globe travel to the "Big Apple" to participate in the world's largest race, the New York City (NYC) Marathon. The running course is an exhausting 26. 2 miles and running the entire race at a slow pace takes about 5 hours— almost an entire school day—of steady running. The NYC Marathon takes place on the first Sunday of November and because of its popularity, participation is limited to 37,000 entrants. Along with the Boston Marathon and Chicago Marathon, it is among the greatest long-distance annual running events in the United States. So how did this popular race get its start?

The NYC Marathon is organized each year by the New York Road Runners club, and the first NYC Marathon was held in 1970. It was organized by the club's presidents, Vince Chiappetta and Fred Lebow. Fred Lebow ran in the foundational NYC Marathon in 1970, finishing 45th with a time of 4:12:09. He was diagnosed with brain cancer in early 1990, and he ran his last NYC Marathon in 1992, in celebration of his 60th birthday. To honor Fred Lebow, a sculpture of him was created in 1994 by an artist named Jesus Ygnacio Dominguez. The sculpture shows Lebow timing runners with his watch.

The first NYC Marathon was a small race with 127 competitors running several loops around a section of Central Park. The entry fee for the race was $1 and a total of 55 runners crossed the finish line. Over the years, the NYC Marathon became more popular and grew larger and larger, and in 1976, Fred Lebow redrew the running course to include all five boroughs of New York City.

The marathon begins on Staten Island near the Verrazano-Narrows Bridge. It winds through Brooklyn for approximately the next eleven miles. After running about two and a half miles in Queens, runners cross the Queensboro Bridge and enter Manhattan. It is at this point in the race when many runners become tired, as the climb up the bridge is considered one of the most difficult pacts in the marathon. Finally reaching Manhattan after about 16 miles, the race proceeds north and crosses briefly into the Bronx before returning to Manhattan. The runners finally race through Central Park to the finish line. In 2000, an official wheelchair and hand cycle division of the marathon was introduced.

The NYC Marathon will celebrate its 40th anniversary in 2009 and the race will include special celebrations. The marathon has always been a focus of community spirit, and more than two million spectators are expected to line the streets for the 2009 race to support the runners.

     LumosLearning.com

21. This passage is

    Ⓐ Nonfiction
    Ⓑ Fiction
    Ⓒ Realistic fiction
    Ⓓ Poetry

22. Who are entrants?

    Ⓐ People who enter a competition.
    Ⓑ People who protest a competition.
    Ⓒ People who exit a competition.
    Ⓓ People who plan a competition.

23. In the passage, why is the running course described as exhausting?

    Ⓐ The race is 26.2 miles.
    Ⓑ At a slow pace it takes about 5 hours to complete.
    Ⓒ It takes more effort to run the race at a faster pace.
    Ⓓ All of these

24. Based on the passage, what did Fred Lebow not do?

    Ⓐ Organize the first NYC Marathon.
    Ⓑ Run in the first NYC Marathon.
    Ⓒ Hire an artist to make a sculpture in his honor.
    Ⓓ Redraw the marathon's running course to include all 5 boroughs of NYC.

25. How many hours did it take for Fred Lebow to complete his first marathon?

    Ⓐ 45 hours
    Ⓑ 4 hours
    Ⓒ 12 hours
    Ⓓ 9 hours

26. A synonym for the word "borough" is

    Ⓐ backyard
    Ⓑ area
    Ⓒ country
    Ⓓ island

27. In what borough does the most difficult part of the running course take place?

   Ⓐ Staten Island
   Ⓑ Bronx
   Ⓒ Queens
   Ⓓ Manhattan

28. According to the passage, after the runners enter Manhattan, they leave briefly to enter what borough?

   Ⓐ Staten Island
   Ⓑ Bronx
   Ⓒ Queens
   Ⓓ Manhattan

29. Who are spectators?

   Ⓐ Racers
   Ⓑ Cheerleaders
   Ⓒ Competitors
   Ⓓ Onlookers

Open-Ended Question 3

30. The NYC Marathon is a very popular race.

- **Describe why you think so many people want to run in the NYC Marathon.**
- **Discuss why proper training and preparation are necessary before running in a marathon.**
- **Explain why you would or would not want to run in the NYC Marathon.**

Reading Task 4

Directions to the Student

Now you will read a story and answer the questions that follow.
Some questions will be multiple-choice; others will be open-ended.

- You may look back at the reading passage as often as you want.
- Read each question carefully and think about the answer and completely fill in the circle next to your choice.
- If you do not know the answer to a question, go on to the next question and come back to the skipped question later.

Colonies

The planet seemed to be emptying. Anyone with any sense was boarding the giant ships, taking off to the newly-discovered colonies. Staying behind on a polluted Earth no longer seemed like an intelligent option for anyone who had any money. This was especially true now that the colonies were a viable option, with breathable air and fertile land.

Miles and Lyle found each other on the third day of the voyage. Both of them were extremely excited. They had gone from boring lives as high school sophomores to something new – space explorers. Sure, the voyage would take a full year, but it would be worth it. They were going somewhere no one had ever been before, except a scout drone – a machine that tested each planet's air, land, and water, and searched for any signs of large animals or intelligent beings.

Miles was happy to get as far from his family as he could, searching the far reaches of the ship and exploring any corner he could find. His father and mother had quarreled a lot during the last months before they had boarded the ship. His father believed that leaving was the only intelligent plan. He didn't want to raise his son on a planet that was killing everyone. Miles' mother argued that the unknown dangers of the colony planets could be even greater. And the cost of the travel had nearly bankrupted them. Miles preferred not to be around when his parents were quarreling. Lyle's situation was different. His father had died a few years earlier, and his mother was in poor health. Lyle liked to stay near her, to check on her and reassure her.

The two boys wandered about, with Lyle often checking back in with this mother. They found the food storage unit on the second day. They had a surreptitious feast of six ice cream bars each, until they were chased out by the head cook. They also found the hydroponic farms, where plants from earth were carefully tended. Here Lyle and Miles were much more careful, caressing the plants lovingly. The head gardener let them wander through the greenery, much of which they had never seen even when they had lived on Earth. But their favorite spot was the peak lookout. This was a small window located directly above the ship's bridge. It didn't really make sense. It was as though the person who had designed the ship had stuck it in at the last moment. The stairway that led up to it was out of the way, and there was nothing else to go to nearby.

For these reasons, Lyle and Miles often found themselves alone in the peak lookout for long hours. They would lie on their bellies, gazing at the stars. At the speeds they were moving, they could see the position of the stars change if they waited for more than ten minutes. When they came back the next day, they would have a whole new star system to stare at. A few times they saw planets – small, round balls that seemed to be welcoming them. Miles sometimes would sneak onto the bridge where the navigation and piloting occurred. Lyle was often concerned about his mother, and would return to her cabin to spend time with her.

At the end of the long year, the ship threw itself into reverse as it began to slow down. They were approaching the colonies. Lyle grew increasingly excited, and talked about almost nothing but the planet they would settle. Miles, though, grew increasingly quiet. He was making a decision that would impact the rest of his life. Even Lyle was surprised when Miles said he wasn't going to join his family on the new planet. He wanted to stay on board and learn to fly the big spaceships.

As Miles and Lyle said goodbye, they knew it wasn't forever. They would see each other again, someday. Lyle joined his mother at the gangplank and stepped out into the cool blue light of the strangely fresh new world. He turned to wave to Miles, but he could no longer see him.

LumosLearning.com

31. Why does the spaceship leave Earth?

  Ⓐ to explore the reaches of space
  Ⓑ because the people on board are wealthy
  Ⓒ to transport colonists
  Ⓓ to train young navigators and pilots

32. Read the following sentence from the story:

  "They had a surreptitious feast of six ice cream bars each, until they were chased out by the head cook."

  What does "surreptitious" mean?

  Ⓐ Stealthy
  Ⓑ Delightful
  Ⓒ Filling
  Ⓓ Illegal

33. What do the colonists know for certain about the new planet?

  Ⓐ It has intelligent creatures they can communicate with.
  Ⓑ It has land that crops can grow on.
  Ⓒ It has air so poisonous they will have to wear helmets.
  Ⓓ It is better than Earth.

34. Which of the following is the best description of Lyle's attitude on board the ship?

  Ⓐ He endures it, but wishes it would end.
  Ⓑ He enjoys it, but is concerned about his mother.
  Ⓒ He is excited by it, and is constantly exploring.
  Ⓓ He likes the thrills of sneaking into the food storage unit best.

35. What would be a good subtitle for this story?

  Ⓐ "The Wealthy Way to Travel"
  Ⓑ "The Colonists"
  Ⓒ "Life on a New Planet"
  Ⓓ "Two Friends, Two Paths"

36. What is the purpose of the drones?

  Ⓐ To grow Earth plants for use upon arrival.
  Ⓑ To pilot the ship when a human being needs a rest.
  Ⓒ To explore possible planets for suitability.
  Ⓓ To be used as a lookout point.

37. Which of the following is NOT a reason Miles likes to spend time at the peak lookout?

Ⓐ to avoid his family
Ⓑ to learn navigation and piloting
Ⓒ to be with his friend Lyle
Ⓓ to see the stars go by

38. Why do Miles' parents disagree with each other?

Ⓐ His father thinks that interstellar travel is dangerous, but his mother does not.
Ⓑ His mother thinks that travel on a spaceship is dangerous, but his father thinks it will be good for Miles.
Ⓒ His father thinks that Earth's pollution is too dangerous, but his mother thinks that the unknown dangers could be worse.
Ⓓ His mother thinks that he will make friends on board the ship, but his father does not think so.

39. Read the following sentence:

"This was especially true now that the colonies were a viable option, with breathable air and fertile land."

What does "viable" mean?

Ⓐ Practical
Ⓑ Interstellar
Ⓒ Inhaled
Ⓓ Traveling

LumosLearning.com

Open-Ended Question 4

Here are some reminders for when you are completing this Open-Ended Question:

- Read the passage "Colonies" and the open-ended question and write your answer on a sheet of paper.
- Focus your response on the question asked.
- Answer all parts of the question and explain your answer with specific details.
- Use specific information from the story to answer all the parts of the question.

40. After reading the above passage:

- **Describe what Miles and Lyle did together on board the spaceship.**
- **Discuss in what ways Miles and Lyle are similar. In what ways are they different?**
- **If you were Miles, would you stay on board the ship? Explain why, or why not?**

End Of Practice Test - 2

LumosLearning.com

Practice Test 2 Answers

Sample Answer for Writing Task 1

A 5-point response should include
- Answers to all parts of the question
- Reference to the text in the response
- Personal comparisons

A day that really stands out in my mind is the day that my little sister, Ella, was born. My mom and dad had been talking about her for so long that I was so excited to finally meet her. I made sure that I knew everything there was to know about being an older brother. They told me how small and beautiful she would be, so I couldn't wait to hold her.

When the time finally came for Ella to join us, my whole family was running around like crazy. My dad was trying to pack a suitcase of clothes for the hospital. My grandma was helping my mom do breathing exercises because she was in labor. There was not much for me to do, so I was just trying to stay out of the way.

When we got to the hospital, I thought Ella would join us right away. We ended up waiting hours and hours for her to come. Some of the time I was bored and some of the time I was excited. I kept looking at the clock to see how much time was passing. Luckily, my grandma brought some cards, so I could play with her because sitting in one dull colored old chair got real boring.

When she finally came, I couldn't believe my eyes. She was small and beautiful just like my parents said she would be. My mom and grandma were both crying, and my dad was so quiet. It seemed like he couldn't believe his eyes. When I had a chance to hold her I felt like the world around me stopped. I was so proud to tell her I was her big brother. It is a day I will never forget.

Related Lumos Online Workbook: Correct Use of Adjectives and Adverbs; Correct Subject-Verb Agreement; Recognize Pronouns; Demonstrate Command of Capitalization; Demonstrate Command of Punctuation; Correct Spelling (CCSS: L.6.1, L.6.2, L.6.3)

Reading Task 1 Answer Key

Question No.	Answer	Related Lumos Online Workbook	CCSS
1	A	Analysis of Key Events and Ideas; Conclusions Drawn from the Text;	RL.6.1
2	A	Analysis of Key Events and Ideas; Conclusions Drawn from the Text;	RL.6.1
3	D	Development of Ideas; Summary of Text	RL.6.2
4	A	Development of Ideas; Summary of Text	RL.6.2
5	D	Use Context Clue to Determine Word Meaning; Use Clues to Determine Multiple-Meaning Words; Use Common Roots and Affixes; Consult Reference Materials	L.6.4
6	B	Comparing Author's Writing to Another	RL.6.9
7	C	Use Context Clue to Determine Word Meaning; Use Clues to Determine Multiple-Meaning Words; Use Common Roots and Affixes; Consult Reference Materials	L.6.4
8	A	Analysis of Key Events and Ideas; Conclusions Drawn from the Text;	RL.6.1
9	C	Figurative Words and Phrases; Connotative Words and Phrases; Meaning of Words and Phrases	RL.6.4

Sample Answer for Open–Ended Question 1

A 4-point response should include:
- Answer to all parts of the question
- Reference to the text in response
- Personal comparisons

There are a few reasons that people may not like Poppa P. People probably don't like Poppa P because he is full of himself. All he does is talk about how great he is, and all the things he is doing. He seems like he likes himself more than anyone else does.

I don't think Poppa P would be a good friend at all. The only reason he would want to be a friend is to have someone to talk to about himself. He probably would not be interested in my life, only his, so that is not the characteristic of a good friend. I would get tired of hearing stories about how great he is all the time.

Poppa P could be more likeable if he were more humble and talked about himself less. If he showed interest in other people, that would help also. He seems to think that the only reason people don't like him is that they are jealous. He doesn't realize it is because he is actually really unlikeable. Poppa P gives a few reasons why people may not like him, but he can change that in the future if he would like.

Related Lumos Online Workbook: Correct Use of Adjectives and Adverbs; Correct Subject-Verb Agreement; Recognize Pronouns; Demonstrate Command of Capitalization; Demonstrate Command of Punctuation; Correct Spelling (CCSS: L.6.1, L.6.2, L.6.3)

Sample Answer for Writing Task 2

A 5-point response should include
- Answers to all parts of the question
- Reference to the text in the response
- Personal comparisons

I think prejudice can be caused by a number of different things. Some people are prejudiced because they had one bad experience with a certain kind of person. Others are prejudiced because their parents taught them to be that way growing up. Others are prejudiced because their friends pressure them to be that way. Whatever the reason, prejudice is always wrong.

Acting on prejudice is always a bad idea. For one it limits your life experience. You never get to know a lot of good people who could add value and love to your life. Also, it makes the other person feel really badly. I know it would hurt me if someone turned away or refused to talk to me before they even knew me. It's not respectful. It could hurt someone's feelings. Also, if you have a little brother or sister who looks up to you, it could cause them to be prejudiced, too.

When people in society continue to have prejudices, it can break communities apart. Groups grow up convinced that they don't like or trust each other. They live their whole lives without opening up to those people or being friends. They miss out on learning about other cultures or meeting really great people. By being prejudiced, they end up teaching others to be that way, too, which makes the cycle carry on even further. Prejudice is something that we should not help grow, but help take away.

Related Lumos Online Workbook: Correct Use of Adjectives and Adverbs; Correct Subject-Verb Agreement; Recognize Pronouns; Demonstrate Command of Capitalization; Demonstrate Command of Punctuation; Correct Spelling (CCSS: L.6.1, L.6.2, L.6.3)

     LumosLearning.com

Reading Task 2 Answer Key

Question No.	Answer	Related Lumos Online Workbook	CCSS
11	A	Determine Technical Meanings; Figurative Words and Phrases; Connotative Words and Phrases	RI.6.4
12	D	Analysis of Key Events and Ideas; Conclusions Drawn from the Text; Determine Technical Meanings; Figurative Words and Phrases; Connotative Words and Phrases	RI.6.1, RI.6.4
13	B	Analysis of Key Events and Ideas; Conclusions Drawn from the Text; Central Idea of the Text; Analysis of Key Events and Ideas; Summary of Text	RI.6.1, RI.6.3
14	C	Central Idea of the Text; Summary of Text;	RI.6.2
15	A	Analysis of Key Events and Ideas; Conclusions Drawn from the Text	RI.6.1
16	C	Central Idea of the Text; Summary of Text; Structure of Text; Central Idea of the Text	RI.6.2, RI.6.5
17	C	Analysis of Key Events and Ideas; Conclusions Drawn from the Text	RI.6.1
18	B	Determine Technical Meanings; Figurative Words and Phrases; Connotative Words and Phrases	RI.6.4
19	C	Determine Technical Meanings; Figurative Words and Phrases; Connotative Words and Phrases	RI.6.4

Sample Answer for Open-Ended Question 2

A 4-point response should include:

- Answers to all parts of the question
- Reference to the text in the response
- Personal comparisons

Everyone hopes to have a best friend, but sometimes you also have frienemies. I have a Frienemy named "Jade." (I am calling her "Jade" because she is in this class and I don't want to make it too obvious who she is.) "Jade" and I have spent most of our lives together. We go to each others houses sometimes when our moms want to see each other. We are "friends" because our moms are friends. That means she knows a lot about me, and I know a lot about her. But really, I don't like her or trust her. I have heard her say mean things about me and then deny it later on. It makes me not want to be very nice to her.

The difference between best friends and worse enemies is night and day, but it is very easy to go from one to the other. Your best friend would never do anything to hurt you. At the same time, if your best friend decides not to be your best friend anymore, she will be able to hurt you or embarrass you even worse than anyone else. She will know all your secrets and all your fears and can tell them to other people so they make fun of you. I think that is how most friendships go from bad to worse.

I don't like the idea of having a Frienemy. It is hard not being able to trust people, and you don't want to always have to worry if they are going to stab you in the back. Once you know that someone is a Frienemy it is a little easier because you know you have to watch yourself around them. The hard part is when you think you are actually friends. Everyone should have a best friend and not worry about a frienemy.

Related Lumos Online Workbook: Correct Use of Adjectives and Adverbs; Correct Subject-Verb Agreement; Recognize Pronouns; Demonstrate Command of Capitalization; Demonstrate Command of Punctuation; Correct Spelling (CCSS: L.6.1, L.6.2, L.6.3)

Reading Task 3 Answer Key

Question No.	Answer	Related Lumos Online Workbook	CCSS
21	B	Analysis of Key Events and Ideas; Conclusions Drawn from the Text	RI.6.1
22	A	Determine Technical Meanings; Figurative Words and Phrases; Connotative Words and Phrases	RI.6.4
23	D	Analysis of Key Events and Ideas; Conclusions Drawn from the Text	RI.6.1
24	C	Structure of Text; Central Idea of the Text	RI.6.5
25	B	Analysis of Key Events and Ideas; Conclusions Drawn from the Text	RI.6.1
26	B	Determine Technical Meanings; Figurative Words and Phrases; Connotative Words and Phrases	RI.6.4
27	C	Analysis of Key Events and Ideas; Conclusions Drawn from the Text	RI.6.1
28	B	Analysis of Key Events and Ideas; Conclusions Drawn from the Text	RI.6.1
29	D	Determine Technical Meanings; Figurative Words and Phrases; Connotative Words and Phrases	RI.6.4

Sample Answer for Open–Ended Question 3

A 4-point response should include:
- Answer to all parts of the question
- Reference to the text in response
- Personal comparisons

I think that so many people want to run in the NYC Marathon because New York is such a cool and popular place. There is such a strong spirit there and people love New York City. I would probably consider it an honor to run just because of that. Not to mention that the course is really challenging.

Proper training is necessary before running in a marathon because 26.2 miles is a really long way to run. The story mentions that it would be like running almost an entire day of school. You would have to be very strong and in shape to be able to do that. You would also have to have enough hydration and nutrition to make sure that you didn't faint during the race.

At the moment I don't think I am ready to run in the NYC Marathon. I would need to train for awhile before I made that kind of commitment. If I do end up being a strong marathon runner, I would definitely consider it. New York is a fun place, and it would be exciting to run with so many other runners and have millions of people cheering me on.

Related Lumos Online Workbook: Correct Use of Adjectives and Adverbs; Correct Subject-Verb Agreement; Recognize Pronouns; Demonstrate Command of Capitalization; Demonstrate Command of Punctuation; Correct Spelling (CCSS: L.6.1, L.6.2, L.6.3)

LumosLearning.com

Reading Task 4 Answer Key

Question No.	Answer	Related Lumos Online Workbook	CCSS
31	C	Analysis of Key Events and Ideas; Conclusions Drawn from the Text;	RL.6.1
32	A	Use Context Clue to Determine Word Meaning; Use Clues to Determine Multiple-Meaning Words; Use Common Roots and Affixes; Consult Reference Materials	L.6.4
33	B	Analysis of Key Events and Ideas; Conclusions Drawn from the Text;	RL.6.1
34	B	Development of Ideas; Summary of Text	RL.6.2
35	D	Development of Ideas; Summary of Text	RL.6.2
36	C	Figurative Words and Phrases; Connotative Words and Phrases; Meaning of Words and Phrases	RL.6.4
37	B	Analysis of Key Events and Ideas; Conclusions Drawn from the Text;	RL.6.1
38	C	Analysis of Key Events and Ideas; Conclusions Drawn from the Text;	RL.6.1
39	A	Use Context Clue to Determine Word Meaning; Use Clues to Determine Multiple-Meaning Words; Use Common Roots and Affixes; Consult Reference Materials	L.6.4

Sample Answer for Open–Ended Question 4

A 4-point response should include:
- Answer to all parts of the question
- Reference to the text in response
- Personal comparisons

When Miles and Lyle were together on the ship, they spent a lot of time exploring the ship and looking outside at the stars and planets. They learned about the hydroponic plants and spent time wandering through them. They seemed to have a lot of fun together.

Miles and Lyle were both young and adventurous. They liked to explore different things and seemed excited by the new opportunities in store for them in the colonies. Lyle was closer to his family, though. He was always checking on his mother. Miles seemed to prefer to be independent and stay further away from his family, and was happier when he had a chance to explore on his own.

If I were Miles, I don't think I would stay on the ship. I know it would be interesting to see how to fly the ship, but I would be too curious to see what the colonies were like. I would also miss my family too much to leave them altogether. I am not sure you can spend your life on a ship forever. Maybe Miles is just trying to escape or avoid his problems by staying there. He seems like he doesn't want to face his family. For that reason I think there is a lot more to this story than what was shared.

Related Lumos Online Workbook: Correct Use of Adjectives and Adverbs; Correct Subject-Verb Agreement; Recognize Pronouns; Demonstrate Command of Capitalization; Demonstrate Command of Punctuation; Correct Spelling (CCSS: L.6.1, L.6.2, L.6.3)

Lumos StepUp™ is an educational app that helps students learn and master grade-level skills in Math and English Language Arts. List of features include,

- Learn Anywhere, Anytime!
- Learn about all the Common Core State Standards.
- Grades 3 - 8 Mathematics and English Language Arts.
- Get instant access to the Common Core State Standards
- One full-length sample practice test in all Grades and Subjects.
- Full Practice Tests, Partial Tests and Standards based Tests.
- 2 Test Modes: Normal mode and Learning mode.
- Learning Mode gives the user a step-by-step explanation if the answer is wrong.
- Access to Online Workbooks (tedBook™).
- Provides ability to directly scan QR Codes
- And, it's Completely FREE!

http://lumoslearning.com/a/apps

Lumoslearning

INCLUDES Online Workbooks!

About Online Workbooks

- When you buy this book, 1 year access to online workbooks included

- Access them anytime from a computer with an internet connection

- Adheres to the New Common Core State Standards

- Includes progress reports

- Instant feedback and self-paced

- Ability to review incorrect answers

- Parents and Teachers can assist in student's learning by reviewing their areas of difficulty

Course Name: Grade 4 Math Prep

Lesson Name:	Correct	Total	% Score	Incorrect
Introduction				
Diagnostic Test		3	0%	3
Number and Numerical Operations				
Workbook - Number Sense	2	10	20%	8
Workbook - Numerical Operations	2	25	8%	23
Workbook - Estimation	1	3	33%	2
Geometry and measurement				
Workbook - Geometric Properties		6	0%	6
Workbook - Transforming Shapes				
Workbook - Coordinate Geometry	1	3	33%	2
Workbook - Units of Measurement				
Workbook - Measuring Geometric Objects	3	10	30%	7
Patterns and algebra				
Workbook - Patterns	7	10	70%	3
Workbook - Functions and relationships				

LESSON NAME: Workbook - Geometric Properties
Elapsed Time: 01:19

Question No. 2
What type of motion is being modeled here?

Select right answer
- ⊙ a translation
- ⊙ a rotation 90° clockwise
- ◉ a rotation 90° counter-clockwise
- ⊙ a reflection

[Previous question] [Next question]

Report Name: Missed Questions
Student Name: Lisa Colbright
Cours Name: Grade 4 Math Prep
Lesson Name: Diagnostic Test

The faces on a number cube are labeled with the numbers 1 through 6. What is the probability of rolling a number greater than 4?

Answer Explanation

(C) On a standard number cube, there are six possible outcomes. Of those outcomes, 2 of them are greater than 4. Thus, the probability of rolling a number greater than 4 is "2 out of 6" or 2/6.

A) 1/6
B) 1/3
C) Correct Answer 2/6
D) 3/6